brother
to
brother

90 DEVOTIONS FOR MEN
ON FAITH AND LIFE

TIM GUSTAFSON

Our Daily Bread
Publishing™

Brother to Brother: 90 Devotions for Men on Faith and Life
© 2022 by Our Daily Bread Ministries

The devotional readings collected in this book were first published over a span of years in the *Our Daily Bread* devotional booklets that are distributed around the world in more than fifty languages.

Requests for permission to quote from this book should be directed to Permissions Department, Our Daily Bread Ministries, PO Box 3566, Grand Rapids, MI 49501, or contact us by email at permissionsdept@odb.org

Scripture quotations, unless otherwise indicated, are taken from the Holy Bible, New International Version®, NIV®. Copyright © 1973, 1978, 1984, 2011 by Biblica, Inc.™ Used by permission of Zondervan. All rights reserved worldwide. www.zondervan.com.
    Scripture quotations marked ESV are taken from the ESV® Bible (The Holy Bible, English Standard Version®), copyright © 2001 by Crossway, a publishing ministry of Good News Publishers. Used by permission. All rights reserved.
    Scripture quotations marked KJV are taken from the Authorized Version, or King James Version, of the Bible.
    Scripture quotations marked NKJV are from the New King James Version®. Copyright © 1982 by Thomas Nelson. Used by permission. All rights reserved.
    Scripture quotations marked NLT are taken from the Holy Bible, New Living Translation, copyright © 1996, 2004, 2015 by Tyndale House Foundation. Used by permission of Tyndale House Publishers, Inc., Carol Stream, Illinois 60188. All rights reserved.

ISBN: 978-1-64070-142-7

Library of Congress Cataloging-in-Publication Data Available

Printed in China
23 24 25 26 27 28 29 30 / 9 8 7 6 5 4 3

brother
to
brother

Oh, the Stories You'll Tell

My brother and I were just five and six years old when Mom and Dad took us to sea—on a freighter! The ship was the *African Lightning*, and it hauled cargo between New York and Africa.

Our parents were missionaries, and this was the most economical way to return to Ghana from the USA. After several stops along Africa's west coast, the ship bypassed our destination of Accra and headed for Nigeria.

The year was 1967. Nigeria was in the throes of the Biafran Civil War. For security reasons, the ship anchored out in Lagos harbor. Each night the ship's lights were darkened due to a mandatory blackout.

Because we couldn't moor pierside, offloading was done via barge—a maddeningly methodical process that took nearly two weeks. Dad knew we'd die of boredom (it's possible when you're six years old) if we stayed on the ship, so each day we boarded a small watercraft and went ashore.

When I tell this story, people ask if I was afraid. The honest answer is no. Not even a little bit. There's a good reason for that.

Dad was a World War II veteran who loved to tell us stories about the war. I knew they were true, because he told them on himself. He told us of the terror he felt during that first moment of combat. (He ran into the woods and hid.) He told of the foolish mistakes he made under duress and of the time when, in a panic, he prayed a foxhole prayer. Dad was never the hero of his own stories.

In Lagos, Nigeria, in 1967, Phil and I weren't afraid because our father wasn't afraid. And we knew that he had known real fear.

Dad showed us what genuine faith looks like. He didn't have all the answers, but he knew who did. Dad didn't fear death because he had a Father who walked with him. That's the most important lesson he taught us.

My brother Phil and I are nine months and one day apart. Mom and Dad adopted us both. Growing up, we were fiercely competitive. As adults, we grew so very proud of each other. Phil is gone now, taken much too soon by a brain aneurysm. But we shared a faith in the same God, and so we enjoy the closest connection brothers can have. It's a bond that can never die. I'll see Phil again. I'll see Mom and Dad too.

Mom, Dad, and my brother are woven into the stories I now tell—including the ones about my own lengthy military career. These days, I strive to pass these stories on to my own children, including my daughter, my seven sons, and our first granddaughter.

My family is the primary reason I've chosen these words of the warrior-poet David as my life verses:

> **Father to the fatherless, defender of widows—**
> **this is God, whose dwelling is holy**
> **God places the lonely in families;**
> **he sets the prisoners free and gives them joy.**
> **—PSALM 68:5–6** NLT

—TIM GUSTAFSON
SENIOR CONTENT EDITOR
OUR DAILY BREAD MINISTRIES

Brother to Brother

GENESIS 33:1–11

～～～～

A new command I give you: Love one another.

—JOHN 13:34

My brother and I, less than a year apart in age, were quite "competitive" growing up (translation: we fought!). Dad understood. He had brothers. Mom? Not so much.

Our story could have fit in the book of Genesis, which might well be subtitled "A Brief History of Sibling Rivalry." Cain and Abel (Genesis 4); Isaac and Ishmael (21:8–10); Joseph and everyone not named Benjamin (chapter 37). But for brother-to-brother animosity, it's hard to beat Jacob and Esau.

Esau's twin brother had cheated him twice, so he wanted to kill Jacob (27:41). Decades later Jacob and Esau would reconcile (chapter 33). But the rivalry continued on in their descendants, who became the nations of Edom and Israel. When the people of Israel prepared to enter the promised land, Edom met them with threats and an army (Numbers 20:14–21). Much later, as Jerusalem's citizens fled invading forces, Edom slaughtered the refugees (Obadiah 1:10–14).

Happily for us, the Bible contains not just the sad account of our brokenness but the story of God's redemption as well. Jesus changed everything, telling His disciples, "A new command I give you: Love one another" (John 13:34). Then He showed us what that means by dying for us.

As my brother and I got older, we became close. That's the thing with God. When we respond to the forgiveness He offers, His grace can transform our sibling rivalries into brotherly love.

MAKING IT WORK

Let's extend this "brother" thing beyond your family. What about the guys at work, the men you encounter at church, even the friends you go to ball games with? Does there need to be some forgiveness happening between you and any one of them? This can apply to both brothers in Christ (fellow believers in Jesus) or just brothers in humanity. God's grace can help when forgiveness is on the agenda.

_____

_____

_____

_____

_____

_____

_____

_____

_____

_____

_____

_____

_____

_____

_____

_____

Strong Conqueror

JOHN 18:10–14, 36–37

~~~~~~~

My kingdom is not of this world.

—JOHN 18:36

Most of us hope for good government. We vote, we serve, and we speak out for causes we believe are fair and just. But political solutions remain powerless to change the condition of our hearts.

Many of Jesus's followers anticipated a Messiah who would bring a vigorous political response to Rome and its heavy-handed oppression. Peter was no exception. When Roman soldiers came to arrest Christ, Peter drew his sword and took a swing at the head of the high priest's servant, lopping off his ear in the process.

Jesus halted Peter's one-man war, saying, "Put your sword away! Shall I not drink the cup the Father has given me?" (John 18:11). Hours later, Jesus would tell Pilate, "My kingdom is not of this world. If it were, my servants would fight to prevent my arrest by the Jewish leaders" (v. 36).

The Lord's restraint in that moment, as His life hung in the balance, astonishes us when we ponder the scope of His mission. On a day yet in the future, He will lead the armies of heaven into battle. John wrote, "With justice he judges and wages war" (Revelation 19:11).

But as He endured the ordeal of His arrest, trial, and crucifixion, Jesus kept His Father's will in view. By embracing death on the cross, He set in motion a chain of events that truly transforms hearts. And in the process, our Strong Conqueror defeated death itself.

MAKING IT WORK

When you trusted Jesus, what did He conquer for you? What do you need Him to help you conquer today? What reminder can you keep with you each day to remind you that He is there beside you to help you conquer life for His glory?

_____

_____

_____

_____

_____

_____

_____

_____

_____

_____

_____

_____

_____

_____

_____

_____

_____

_____

_____

Impossible?

MATTHEW 5:38–42

~~~~~~~~~~

You have heard that it was said, "Eye for eye, and tooth for tooth." But I tell you, do not resist an evil person.

— MATTHEW 5:38–39

When Nobel Prize Chairman Gunnar John delivered his presentation speech for Martin Luther King's 1964 Peace Prize, he quoted Jesus: "Whosoever shall smite thee on thy right cheek, turn to him the other also" (Matthew 5:39 KJV). As Mr. John noted: "It was not because he led a racial minority in their struggle for equality that Martin Luther King achieved fame. . . . [His] name will endure for the way in which he has waged his struggle."

In 1955, King had led a yearlong, peaceful boycott to protest segregation on buses. He paid a high price. His home was bombed, and he was assaulted and arrested. He never retaliated. Eventually, in 1968, he was assassinated.

How contrary Dr. King's peaceful example stands to my fleshly nature! I want justice now. I want retribution. I want others to pay for their wrongdoing, especially when it's directed at me. What I do not want is to turn the other cheek and invite them to take another swing.

Haddon Robinson comments on the lofty standards Jesus set forth in the Sermon on the Mount (Matthew 5–7), calling them "goals . . . not impossible ideals. [Jesus] wants His disciples to strive toward these goals to master a new kind of life."

Amid the injustices of life, may we have the courage, faith, and strength to turn the other cheek.

MAKING IT WORK

Turning the other cheek doesn't sound like the action of a hero. But it is. What does this kind of action defeat in the realm of personal relationships? Can you think of ways using Jesus's principle that can help you turn a possible defeat in a relationship with someone else into a victory in His name?

_____

_____

_____

_____

_____

_____

_____

_____

_____

_____

_____

_____

_____

_____

_____

_____

_____

An Exchange

PSALM 32:1–11

～～～～

I said, "I will confess my transgressions to the LORD."
And you forgave the guilt of my sin.

—PSALM 32:5

Jen sat on her patio pondering a scary question: Should she write a book? She had enjoyed writing a blog and speaking in public, but she felt that God might want her to do more. "I asked God if He wanted me to do this," she said. She talked with Him and asked for His leading.

She began to wonder if God wanted her to write about her husband's pornography addiction and how God was working in his life and their marriage. But then she thought that it might publicly disrespect him. So she prayed, "What if we wrote it together?" and she asked her husband Craig. He agreed to help her with the book project.

While King David didn't say what sin he is referring to in Psalm 32, he engaged in a public conversation about his struggles. He even put them into song. "When I kept silent, my bones wasted away," he wrote (Psalm 32:3). So he said, "I will confess my transgressions to the LORD" (v. 5). Not everyone should go public with their private battles. But when David confessed his sin, he found peace and healing that inspired him to worship God.

Craig and Jen say that the process of writing their deeply personal story has brought them closer than ever. God loves to exchange our guilt, shame, and isolation for His forgiveness, courage, and community!

MAKING IT WORK

Rarely is anything valuable accomplished on our own. We need the strength of fellow believers who can speak God's truth into our lives and coach us through our ventures—no matter what form that venture takes. Do you have a situation for which you need some human assistance? Why not get together with this friend and see if the two of you can conquer this challenge together?

_____

_____

_____

_____

_____

_____

_____

_____

_____

_____

_____

_____

_____

_____

_____

Something New

EPHESIANS 2:10–22

~~~~~~~~

We are God's handiwork, created in Christ Jesus to do good works, which God prepared in advance for us to do.

—EPHESIANS 2:10

It was only scrap wood, but Charles Hooper saw much more than that. Salvaging old timbers from a long-abandoned corncrib, he sketched some simple plans. Then he felled a few oak and poplar trees from his wooded property and painstakingly squared them with his grandfather's broadax. Piece by piece, he began to fit together the old lumber with the new.

Today you can see Charles and Shirley Hooper's postcard-perfect log cabin, tucked away in the trees on Tennessee Ridge. Part guesthouse, part museum for family heirlooms, the structure stands as an enduring tribute to Charles's vision, skill, and patience.

Writing to a Gentile audience, Paul told the church at Ephesus how Jesus was creating something new by bringing together Jewish and non-Jewish believers as a single entity. "You who once were far away have been brought near by the blood of Christ," Paul wrote (Ephesians 2:13). This new structure was "built on the foundation of the apostles and prophets, with Christ Jesus himself as the chief cornerstone. In him the whole building is joined together and rises to become a holy temple in the Lord" (vv. 20–21).

The work continues today. God takes the brokenness of our lives, artfully fits us together with other broken and rescued people, and patiently chips away our rough edges. He loves His work, you know.

MAKING IT WORK

What do you feel Jesus created in you for His glory? How can you take the building materials of your life as it is right now and build something new and worthwhile for Christ's kingdom?

_____

_____

_____

_____

_____

_____

_____

_____

_____

_____

_____

_____

_____

_____

_____

_____

_____

_____

Web Wisdom

PROVERBS 26:1–12

~~~~~~~

A quarrelsome person starts fights as easily as
hot embers light charcoal or fire lights wood.

— **PROVERBS 26:21** NLT

Scroll to the bottom of many online news sites, and you'll find the "Comments" section where readers can leave their observations. Even the most reputable sites have no shortage of rude rants, uninformed insults, and name-calling.

The book of Proverbs was collected about three thousand years ago, but its timeless wisdom is as up-to-date as today's breaking news. Two proverbs in chapter 26 seem at first glance to contradict each other, yet they apply perfectly to social media. "Do not answer a fool according to his folly, lest you also be like him" (v. 4 NKJV). And then, "Answer a fool according to his folly, lest he be wise in his own eyes" (v. 5 NKJV).

The balance in those statements is in the "according to": Don't answer in the way a fool would answer. But respond so that foolishness is not considered wisdom.

My problem is that the foolishness I encounter is often my own. I have at times posted a sarcastic comment or turned someone else's statement back on them. God hates it when I treat my fellow human beings with such disrespect, even when they're also being foolish.

God gives us an amazing range of freedoms. We are free to choose what we will say, and when and how we say it. And we are always free to ask Him for wisdom.

MAKING IT WORK

Handling social media properly has become a problem for many followers of Jesus. We want to make our feelings known, but we sometimes leave our Christian grace behind when we get on the keyboard. What are three guidelines you can develop for your devices to remind yourself to be Christlike at all times when you're on social media?

_____

_____

_____

_____

_____

_____

_____

_____

_____

_____

_____

_____

_____

_____

_____

_____

_____

Fault Lines

ACTS 6:1–7

~~~~~~~~

*They presented these men to the apostles, who prayed
and laid their hands on them. So the word of God spread.*

—ACTS 6:6–7

An influx of refugees to our community has led to new growth
in area churches. That growth brings challenges. Church members must learn how to welcome these newcomers as they adjust
to a strange culture, new language, and different worship styles.
All this change can create some awkward situations.

Misunderstandings and disagreements occur everywhere we
find people. Church is no exception. If we don't handle our
differences in a healthy way, they can harden into divisions.

The early church in Jerusalem was growing when a dispute
arose that broke along a cultural fault line. The Greek-speaking
Jews (the Hellenists) had a complaint against those Jews who
spoke Aramaic. The Hellenist widows "were being overlooked
in the daily distribution of food" (Acts 6:1). So the apostles
said, "Choose seven men from among you who are known to
be full of the Spirit and wisdom" (v. 3). The seven chosen all
had Greek names (v. 5). In other words, they were Hellenists,
members of the group being neglected. They best understood

the problem. The apostles prayed over them and the church thrived (vv. 6–7).

Growth brings challenges, in part because it increases interactions across traditional barriers. But as we seek the Holy Spirit's guidance, we'll find creative solutions as potential problems turn into opportunities for more growth.

MAKING IT WORK

What are the top three challenges in your sphere of influence? What is your approach to those situations? Benign neglect, prayerful consideration, active involvement, or aggressive leadership? How can you allow the Holy Spirit to guide you in these matters?

_____

_____

_____

_____

_____

_____

_____

_____

_____

_____

_____

_____

_____

_____

_____

_____

_____

_____

~~~~~~~~

"Misunderstandings and disagreements occur everywhere we find people. Church is no exception."

~~~~~~~~

Go Fever

NUMBERS 14:39–45

~~~~~~~~

Be still before the Lord and wait patiently for him.

— PSALM 37:7

On January 28, 1986, after five weather-related delays, the space shuttle *Challenger* lumbered heavenward amid a thunderous overture of noise and flame. A mere seventy-three seconds later, a system failure tore the shuttle apart, and all seven crewmembers perished.

The disaster was attributed to an O-ring seal known to have vulnerabilities. Insiders referred to the fatal mistake as "go fever"—the tendency to ignore vital precautions in the rush to a grand goal.

Our ambitious human nature relentlessly tempts us to make ill-advised choices. Yet we are also prone to a fear that can make us overly cautious. The ancient Israelites demonstrated both traits. When the twelve scouts returned from spying out the Promised Land, ten of the twelve saw only the obstacles (Numbers 13:26–33). "We can't attack those people; they are stronger than we are," they said (v. 31). After a fearful rebellion against the Lord, the people suddenly developed a case of "go fever." They said, "Now we are ready to go up to the land the Lord promised" (14:40).

Without God, the ill-timed invasion failed miserably (vv. 41–45).

When we take our eyes off the Lord, we'll slide into one of two extremes. We'll impatiently rush ahead without Him, or we'll cower and complain in fear. Focusing on Him brings courage tempered with His wisdom.

MAKING IT WORK

Think about the two extremes in the last paragraph. Which of the two most often describes you? How can the words of Psalm 37:7 help get you on the right track with your timing in life?

_____

_____

_____

_____

_____

_____

_____

_____

_____

_____

_____

_____

_____

_____

_____

_____

_____

_____

_____

The Mighty Finns

ISAIAH 37:30–38

~~~~~~~~

LORD our God, deliver us from his hand, so that all the kingdoms of the earth may know that you, LORD, are the only God.

— ISAIAH 37:20

It began as a distant, foreboding hum, then grew into an ominous, earth-rattling din. Soon hundreds of tanks and thousands of enemy infantrymen swarmed into view of the badly outnumbered soldiers in Finland. Assessing the murderous wave, an anonymous Finn lent some perspective. Courageously, he wondered aloud about the enemy: "Where will we find room to bury them all?"

Some 2,600 years before Finland showed such pluck in that World War II battle, an anxious Judean citizenry reacted quite differently to their own overwhelming situation. The Assyrian armies had trapped the people of Jerusalem inside its walls, where they faced the hopeless prospect of a starvation-inducing siege. Hezekiah nearly panicked. But then he prayed, "LORD Almighty, the God of Israel, enthroned between the cherubim, you alone are God over all the kingdoms of the earth" (Isaiah 37:16).

Through the prophet Isaiah, the Lord answered with strong words for Assyria's King Sennacherib. "Against whom have you raised your voice and lifted your eyes in pride? Against the Holy

One of Israel!" (v. 23). Then God comforted Jerusalem. "I will defend this city and save it, for my sake and for the sake of David my servant!" (v. 35). The Lord defeated Sennacherib and destroyed the Assyrian army (vv. 36–38).

No matter what dangers loom on your horizon today, the God of Hezekiah and Isaiah still reigns. He longs to hear from each of us and show himself powerful.

MAKING IT WORK

What are the dangers and worries that wake you up in the night? How has God equipped you to handle them? How often do you ask for God's help with those tough challenges?

_____

_____

_____

_____

_____

_____

_____

_____

_____

_____

_____

_____

_____

_____

_____

_____

_____

_____

Leave a Legacy

2 CHRONICLES 21:4–20

～～～～

Even the Son of Man did not come to be served, but to serve.

—MARK 10:45

When a road-construction foreman was killed in an accident, the love of this man for his family, coworkers, and community resulted in an overwhelming sense of loss. His country church couldn't accommodate all the mourners, so planners moved the service to a much larger building. Friends and family packed the auditorium! The message was clear: Tim touched many lives in a way uniquely his. So many would miss his kindness, sense of humor, and enthusiasm for life.

As I returned from the funeral, I thought about the Scripture passage I had read that morning telling of the life of King Jehoram. What a contrast! His brief reign of terror is traced in 2 Chronicles 21. To solidify his power, Jehoram killed his own brothers and other leaders (v. 4). Then he led Judah into idol worship. The record tells us, "He passed away, to no one's regret" (v. 20). Jehoram thought that brute force would ensure his legacy. It did. He is forever commemorated in Scripture as an evil man and a self-centered leader.

Although Jesus also was a king, He came to Earth to be a servant. As He went about doing good, He endured the hatred of those who grasped for power. In the process, this Servant-King gave His life away.

Today, Jesus lives, as does His legacy. That legacy includes those who understand that life isn't just about themselves. It's about Jesus—the One who longs to wrap His strong, forgiving arms around anyone who turns to Him.

MAKING IT WORK

As things stand right now, what do you think your legacy will be? What would be the top few things people would say about you? Is serving others in Jesus's name in that list? What an example Jesus set for us!

_____

_____

_____

_____

_____

_____

_____

_____

_____

_____

_____

_____

_____

_____

_____

_____

_____

_____

_____

No Outsiders

DEUTERONOMY 10:12–22

～～～～

*What does the Lord your God ask of you but to fear the
Lord your God, to walk in obedience to him, to love him.*

— DEUTERONOMY 10:12

In the remote region of Ghana where I lived as a boy, "Chop time,
no friend" was a common proverb. It was a humorous way of
acknowledging the fact that food in certain areas was scarce, and
Ghanaians are by nature very giving people. Were you to walk in,
they might well give you the last of their food.

In the Philippines, where I also lived for a time, if you visit
unannounced at mealtime, your hosts will insist on sharing with
you regardless of whether they have enough for themselves.

As the Israelites left Egypt, God provided specific instructions to govern their culture. But rules—even God's rules—can
never change hearts. So Moses said, "Change your hearts and
stop being stubborn" (Deuteronomy 10:16 NLT). Interestingly,
right after issuing that challenge Moses took up the topic of Israel's treatment of outsiders. God "loves the foreigner residing
among you," he said, "giving them food and clothing. And you
are to love those who are foreigners, for you yourselves were foreigners in Egypt" (vv. 18–19).

Israel served the "God of gods and Lord of lords, the great God, mighty and awesome" (v. 17). One powerful way they were to show their identification with God was by loving foreigners—those from outside their culture.

What might this small picture of God's character mean for us today? How can we show His love to the marginalized and the needy in our world?

MAKING IT WORK

Who are the outsiders in your world? Realizing that they are made in God's image and Jesus died for them, is there any reason they should not be treated with love and compassion?

_____

_____

_____

_____

_____

_____

_____

_____

_____

_____

_____

_____

_____

_____

_____

_____

_____

_____

Officer Miglio's Heart

MATTHEW 18:1–10

~~~~~

See that you do not despise one of these little ones.
For I tell you that their angels in heaven
always see the face of my Father in heaven.

—MATTHEW 18:10

Back at the police station, Officer Miglio slumped wearily against a wall. A domestic violence call had just consumed half his shift. Its aftermath left a boyfriend in custody, a young daughter in the emergency room, and a shaken mother wondering how it had come to this. This call would wear on the young officer for a long time.

"Nothing you could do, Vic," said his sergeant sympathetically. But the words rang hollow. Some police officers seem able to leave their work at work. Not Vic Miglio. Not the tough cases like this one.

Officer Miglio's heart reflects the compassion of Jesus. Christ's disciples had just come to Him with a question: "Who, then, is the greatest in the kingdom of heaven?" (Matthew 18:1). Calling a small child to Him, He told His disciples, "Unless you change and become like little children, you will never enter the kingdom of heaven" (v. 3). Then He gave a stern warning to anyone who would harm a child (v. 6). In fact, children are so special to Him that Jesus told us, "Their angels in heaven always see the face of my Father in heaven" (v. 10).

How comforting, then, that Jesus's love for children is connected to His love for us all! That's why He invites us, through childlike faith, to become His sons and daughters.

MAKING IT WORK

Consider the many ways you can serve children. One is by coaching them in a sport you are familiar with. Perhaps you could think of other ways to use the skills and abilities you have to serve kids.

_____

_____

_____

_____

_____

_____

_____

_____

_____

_____

_____

_____

_____

_____

_____

_____

_____

_____

_____

Stories in a Cabin

HEBREWS 9:11–15

~~~~~~~

[Christ] went through the greater and more perfect tabernacle that is not made with human hands.

— HEBREWS 9:11

The vintage cabin, expertly constructed from hand-hewn logs, was worthy of a magazine cover. But the structure itself was only half the treasure. Inside, family heirlooms clung to the walls, infusing the home with memories. On the table sat a hand-woven egg basket, an ancient biscuit board, and an oil lamp. A weathered pork pie hat perched over the front door. "There's a story behind everything," the proud owner said.

When God gave Moses instructions for constructing the tabernacle, there was a "story" behind everything (Exodus 25–27). The tabernacle had only one entrance, just as we have only one way to God (see Acts 4:12). The thick inner curtain separated the people from the Most Holy Place where God's presence dwelt: Our sin separates us from God. Inside the Most Holy Place was the ark of the covenant, which symbolized God's presence. The high priest was a forerunner of the greater Priest to come—Jesus himself. The blood of the sacrifices foreshadowed Christ's perfect sacrifice: "He entered the Most Holy Place once for all by his own blood, thus obtaining eternal redemption" (Hebrews 9:12).

All these things told the story of Christ and the work He would accomplish on our behalf. He did it so that "those who are called may receive the promised eternal inheritance" (v. 15). Jesus invites us to be a part of His story.

MAKING IT WORK

This is the key question for all of humanity, whether they know it or not. Are you a part of Jesus's story? Have you trusted Him by faith, knowing that He can forgive your sins because of His death, burial, and resurrection—providing an "eternal inheritance"? It's the most important question you'll ever be asked.

_____

_____

_____

_____

_____

_____

_____

_____

_____

_____

_____

_____

_____

_____

_____

_____

_____

_____

The Tyranny of the Perfect

1 JOHN 1:5–2:2

~~~~~~

*If we claim to be without sin, we deceive ourselves
and the truth is not in us.*

— 1 JOHN 1:8

Dr. Brian Goldman obsessively tried to be perfect in treating his patients. But on a nationally broadcast show he admitted to mistakes he had made. He revealed that he had treated a woman in the emergency room and then made the decision to discharge her. Later that day a nurse asked him, "Do you remember that patient you sent home? Well, she's back." The patient had been readmitted to the hospital and then died. This devastated him. He tried even harder to be perfect, only to learn the obvious: Perfection is impossible.

As Christians, we may harbor unrealistic expectations of perfection for ourselves. But even if we can somehow manage the appearance of a flawless life, our thoughts and motives are never completely pure.

John the disciple wrote, "If we claim to be without sin, we deceive ourselves and the truth is not in us" (1 John 1:8). The remedy is not to hide our sins and to strive harder, but to step into the light of God's truth and confess them. "If we walk in the light," said

John, "as he is in the light, we have fellowship with one another, and the blood of Jesus, his Son, purifies us from all sin" (v. 7).

In medicine, Dr. Goldman proposes the idea of a "redefined physician" who—in a culture where we are hesitant to admit our errors—no longer toils under the tyranny of perfection. Such a physician openly shares mistakes and supports colleagues who do the same, with a goal of reducing mistakes.

What if Christians were known not for hiding their sins but for loving and supporting each other with the truth and grace of our God? What if we practiced a risky yet healthy honesty with each other and with the watching world?

MAKING IT WORK

What in this article resonates with you—the search for perfection or the hiding of sin? The two are related. We know we aren't perfect, and we know we sin. How can you keep both realities in front of you to produce a more godly life?

_____

_____

_____

_____

_____

_____

_____

_____

_____

_____

_____

_____

Tissue Boxes

PSALM 31:9–18

~~~~~~~

I trust in you, LORD; I say, "You are my God."
My times are in your hands.

—PSALM 31:14–15

As I sat in the surgical waiting room, I had time to think. I had been here recently, when we received the jarring news that my only brother, much too young, was "brain dead."

And so on this day, waiting for news about my wife, who was undergoing a serious surgical procedure, I penned a lengthy note to her. Then, surrounded by nervous chatter and oblivious children, I listened for the quiet voice of God.

Suddenly, news! The surgeon wanted to see me. I went to a secluded room to wait. There, on the table, sat two tissue boxes, conspicuously available. They weren't for the sniffles. They were for cold, hard phrases like I heard when my brother died—"brain dead" and "nothing we can do."

In such times of grief or uncertainty, the honesty of the psalms makes them a natural place to turn. Psalm 31 was the heart-cry of David, who endured so much that he wrote, "My life is consumed by anguish" (v. 10). Compounding that grief was the pain of abandonment by his friends and neighbors (v. 11).

But David had the bedrock of faith in the one true God. "I trust in you, LORD; I say, 'You are my God.' My times are in your hands" (vv. 14–15). His lament concludes with resounding encouragement and hope. "Be strong and take heart, all you who hope in the LORD" (v. 24).

This time in the waiting room, the surgeon gave us good news: My wife could expect a full and complete recovery. Of course we're relieved and grateful! But even if she hadn't been "okay," our times still remain in God's capable hands.

MAKING IT WORK

Think about a time when you got bad news about a loved one. How did knowing God help you and give you hope? Is He with us just when there is good news—or is He there either way?

_____

_____

_____

_____

_____

_____

_____

_____

_____

_____

_____

_____

_____

_____

_____

A Tree To Heal

GENESIS 3:1–11

Have you eaten from the tree that
I commanded you not to eat from?

— GENESIS 3:11

For $300,000, you can buy a new McLaren 720S sports car. The vehicle comes with a V8 engine pumping 710 horsepower— considerably more than you'll need for your morning commute.

Of course, you might be tempted to use all that power. One Virginia driver learned his McLaren was so fast it could go from an upscale showroom to the scrap heap in just twenty-four hours! One day after buying the car, he slammed it into a tree. (Thankfully, he survived.)

Just three chapters into the story of the Bible, we learn how a different bad choice and a tree marred God's good creation. Adam and Eve ate from the one tree they were instructed to leave alone (Genesis 3:11). The story had barely begun, and paradise was already cursed (vv. 14–19).

Another tree would play a role in undoing this curse— the cross Jesus endured on our behalf. His death purchased our future with Him (Deuteronomy 21:23; Galatians 3:13).

The story comes full circle in the Bible's last chapter. There we read of "the tree of life" growing beside the "river of the water of life" (Revelation 22:1–2). As John describes it, this tree will be "for the healing of the nations" (v. 2). And he assures us, "No longer will there be any curse" (v. 3). God's story comes with the happily-ever-after we all long for.

MAKING IT WORK

Owning a car like that McLaren 720S sounds like a dream come true. But it is nothing compared with the reality of what God has in store for those who have put their faith in Him. What about knowing Christ as Savior gives you joy and peace?

_____

_____

_____

_____

_____

_____

_____

_____

_____

_____

_____

_____

_____

_____

_____

_____

_____

_____

Lurking Lions

NUMBERS 14:1–9

~~~~~~~~

The LORD is with us. Do not be afraid of them.

—NUMBERS 14:9

When I was young, my dad would "scare" us by hiding in the bush and growling like a lion. Even though we lived in rural Ghana in the 1960s, it was almost impossible that a lion lurked nearby. My brother and I would laugh and seek out the source of the noise, thrilled that playtime with Dad had arrived.

One day a young friend came for a visit. As we played, we heard the familiar growl. Our friend screamed and ran. My brother and I knew the sound of our father's voice—any "danger" was merely a phantom lion—but a funny thing happened. We ran with her. My dad felt terrible that our friend had been frightened, and my brother and I learned not to be influenced by the panicked reaction of others.

Caleb and Joshua stand out as men unfazed by the panic of others. As Israel was poised to enter the promised land, Moses commissioned twelve scouts to spy out the region. They all saw a beautiful territory, but ten focused on the obstacles and discouraged the entire nation (Numbers 13:27–33). In the process, they started a panic (14:1–4). Only Caleb and Joshua accurately assessed the situation (vv. 6–9). They knew the history of their Father and trusted Him to bring them success.

Some "lions" pose a genuine threat. Others are phantoms. Regardless, as followers of Jesus our confidence is in the One whose voice and deeds we know and trust.

MAKING IT WORK

In real, practical terms, how does knowing Jesus give us confidence to do what we know we should do? What are some "lions" that keep you from moving ahead when you know you should? How can your faith help you fight those fears?

_____

_____

_____

_____

_____

_____

_____

_____

_____

_____

_____

_____

_____

_____

_____

_____

_____

_____

_____

That Thing You Do

2 CHRONICLES 13:10–18

~~~~~~~~

*The people of Judah were victorious because they relied
on the Lord, the God of their ancestors.*

— 2 CHRONICLES 13:18

As the convoy waited to roll out, a young marine rapped urgently
on the window of his team leader's vehicle. Irritated, the sergeant
rolled down his window. "What?"

"You gotta do that thing," the marine said. "What thing?" asked
the sergeant. "You know, that thing you do," replied the marine.

Then it dawned on the sergeant. He always prayed for the convoy's safety, but today he'd been running late and had skipped the
prayer. So he dutifully climbed out of the Humvee and prayed for
his marines. The marine understood the value of his praying leader.

In ancient Judah, Abijah doesn't stand out as a great king. First
Kings 15:3 tells us, "His heart was not fully devoted to the Lord
his God." But as Judah prepared for war against Israel, outnumbered two to one, Abijah knew this much: Faithful people in his
kingdom of Judah had continued worshiping God (2 Chronicles
13:10–12). By contrast, the other ten tribes of Israel had driven out
the priests of God and worshiped pagan gods instead (vv. 8–9). So
Abijah turned confidently to the one true God.

Surely Abijah's checkered history had caused grave damage. But he knew where to turn in the crisis, and his army won soundly "because they relied on the LORD, the God of their ancestors" (v. 18). Our God welcomes whoever comes to Him and relies on Him. It's not too late to turn to Him.

MAKING IT WORK

Are there times when you think: *God doesn't want to hear from me; I've really messed up recently?* Perhaps there is a sense in which you have to ask forgiveness (1 John 1:9), but isn't it a comfort to know that God does want to hear from you? Does He need to hear from you right now?

_____

_____

_____

_____

_____

_____

_____

_____

_____

_____

_____

_____

_____

_____

_____

_____

_____

_____

Out of the Ruins

LAMENTATIONS 5:8–22

*He has granted us new life to rebuild
the house of our God and repair its ruins.*

— EZRA 9:9

In the Jewish Quarter of Jerusalem you'll find Tiferet Yisrael Synagogue. Built in the nineteenth century, the synagogue was dynamited by commandos during the 1948 Arab-Israeli War.

For years the site lay in ruins. Then, in 2014, rebuilding began. As city officials set a piece of rubble as the cornerstone, one of them quoted from Lamentations: "Restore us to yourself, Lord, that we may return; renew our days as of old" (5:21).

Lamentations is Jeremiah's funeral song for Jerusalem. With graphic imagery the prophet describes the impact of war on his city. Verse 21 is his heartfelt prayer for God to intervene. Still, the prophet wonders if that is even possible. He concludes his anguished song with this fearful caveat: "unless you have utterly rejected us and are angry with us beyond measure" (v. 22). Decades later, God did answer that prayer as the exiles returned to Jerusalem.

Our lives too may seem to be in ruins. Troubles of our own making and conflicts we can't avoid may leave us devastated. But we have a Father who understands. Gently, patiently, He clears away the rubble, repurposes it, and builds something better. It takes time, but we can always trust Him. He specializes in rebuilding projects.

Lord, you have reclaimed us, and you are remaking us. Thank you for your love and your care despite our self-centered and destructive ways.

MAKING IT WORK

Has life left you devastated in any way? Why not turn things over to the Lord, trust His goodness and power, and allow Him to give you hope and reconstruction?

_____

_____

_____

_____

_____

_____

_____

_____

_____

_____

_____

_____

_____

_____

_____

_____

_____

_____

How To Wait

PSALM 27:1–3, 7–14

~~~~~~~~~

Hear my voice when I call, LORD;
be merciful to me and answer me.

PSALM 27:7

Frustrated and disappointed with church, seventeen-year-old Trevor began a years-long quest for answers. But nothing he explored seemed to satisfy his longings or answer his questions.

His journey did draw him closer to his parents. Still, he had problems with Christianity. During one discussion, he exclaimed bitterly, "The Bible is full of empty promises."

Another man faced disappointment and hardship that fueled his doubts. But as David fled from enemies who sought to kill him, his response was not to run from God but to praise Him. "Though war break out against me, even then I will be confident," he sang (Psalm 27:3).

Yet David's poem still hints at doubt. His cry, "Be merciful to me and answer me" (v. 7), sounds like a man with fears and questions. "Do not hide your face from me," David pleaded. "Do not reject me or forsake me" (v. 9).

David didn't let his doubts paralyze him, however. Even in those doubts, he declared, "I will see the goodness of the LORD in the land of the living" (v. 13). Then he addressed his readers: you, me, and the Trevors of this world. "Wait for the LORD; be strong and take heart and wait for the LORD" (v. 14).

We won't find fast, simple answers to our huge questions. But we will find—when we wait for Him—a God who can be trusted.

MAKING IT WORK

What are some doubts that trouble you about Christianity? Do they feel like deal breakers, or do you feel that you just need some additional information or teaching? Could there be a trusted Christian leader who could direct you to a source that may help you resolve those doubts?

_____

_____

_____

_____

_____

_____

_____

_____

_____

_____

_____

_____

_____

_____

_____

_____

_____

_____

_____

The Slow Walk

JOB 16:1–5

~~~~~~~~~

I will ask the Father, and he will give you another
advocate to help you and be with you forever.

—JOHN 14:16

Caleb was sick. Really sick! Diagnosed with a nervous system disease, the five-year-old suffered from temporary paralysis. His anxious parents prayed. And waited. Slowly, Caleb began to recover. Months later, when doctors cleared him to attend school, all Caleb could manage was a slow, unsteady walk.

One day his dad visited him at school. He watched his son haltingly descend the steps to the playground. And then he saw Caleb's young friend Tyler come alongside him. For the entire recess, as the other kids raced and romped and played, Tyler slowly walked the playground with his frail friend.

Job must have ached for a friend like Tyler. Instead, he had three friends who were certain that his painful circumstances were caused by his own sins. "Who, being innocent, has ever perished?" asked Eliphaz (Job 4:7). Such accusations prompted Job to bitterly declare, "Miserable comforters, all of you!" (16:2).

How unlike Jesus. On the eve of His crucifixion, He took time to comfort His disciples. He promised them the Holy Spirit, who would be with them forever (John 14:16), and He assured them, "I will not leave you orphans; I will come to you" (v. 18). Then, just before He returned to His Father, He said, "I am with you always, to the very end of the age" (Matthew 28:20).

The One who died for us also walks with us, step by painstaking step.

MAKING IT WORK

As this story indicates, it sometimes takes two (three, really, with Jesus) to accomplish something great for God's glory. Can you think of someone who needs you to "slow walk" with him to achieve a valuable goal for the Lord? Why not talk to that person and find how the two of you can reach a valuable goal?

_____

_____

_____

_____

_____

_____

_____

_____

_____

_____

_____

_____

_____

_____

_____

_____

_____

_____

~~~~~~~

"The One who died for us
also walks with us,
step by painstaking step."

~~~~~~~

Minister of Reconciliation

2 CORINTHIANS 5:16–21

~~~~~~

*While we were God's enemies, we were reconciled
to him through the death of his Son.*

—ROMANS 5:10

As Dr. Martin Luther King Jr. preached on a Sunday morning in 1957, he fought the temptation to retaliate against a society steeped in racism.

"How do you go about loving your enemies?" he asked the Dexter Avenue Baptist congregation in Montgomery, Alabama. "Begin with yourself. . . . When the opportunity presents itself for you to defeat your enemy, that is the time which you must not do it."

Quoting from the words of Jesus, King said: "Love your enemies, bless them that curse you, do good to them that hate you, and pray for them which despitefully use you . . . ; that ye may be the children of your Father which is in heaven" (Matthew 5:44–45 KJV).

As we consider those who harm us, we are wise to remember our former status as enemies of God (see Romans 5:10). But "[God] reconciled us to himself through Christ and gave us the ministry of reconciliation," wrote Paul (2 Corinthians 5:18). Now we have a holy obligation. "He has committed to us the message of reconciliation" (v. 19). We are to take that message to the world.

Racial and political tensions are nothing new. But the business of the church is never to feed divisiveness. We should not attack those unlike us or those who hold different opinions or even those who seek our destruction. Ours is a "ministry of reconciliation" that imitates the selfless servant-heart of Jesus.

MAKING IT WORK

As a recipient of God's reconciliation (taking us from being sinners separated from Him to being His well-loved sons and daughters) how should we treat all other people—regardless of our differences? What kind of person did Jesus love when He was on earth? Ask yourself: Do I love others as He did?

_____

_____

_____

_____

_____

_____

_____

_____

_____

_____

_____

_____

_____

_____

_____

_____

Beyond Disappointment

GENESIS 29:14–30

~~~~~~

Hope in the LORD and keep his way.

— PSALM 37:34

Perhaps you've seen the video of the little boy who learns he's getting another sister. In the middle of his meltdown he laments, "It's always girls, girls, girls, girls!"

The story gives an amusing glimpse into human expectations, but there's nothing funny about disappointment. It saturates our world. One story from the Bible seems especially steeped in disappointment. Jacob agreed to work seven years for the right to marry his boss's daughter Rachel. But after fulfilling his contract, Jacob got a wedding night surprise. In the morning he discovered not Rachel but her sister Leah.

We focus on Jacob's disappointment, but imagine how Leah must have felt! What hopes and dreams of hers began to die that day as she was forced to marry a man who did not love or want her?

Psalm 37:4 tells us, "Take delight in the LORD, and he will give you the desires of your heart." Are we to believe that God-fearing people are never disappointed? No, the psalm clearly shows that the writer sees injustice all around him. But he takes the long view:

"Be still before the Lord and wait patiently for him" (v. 7). His conclusion: "The meek will inherit the land" (v. 11).

In the end, it was Leah whom Jacob honored. Eventually the two of them were buried in the family grave plot with Abraham and Sarah, Isaac and Rebekah (Genesis 49:31). And it was through the lineage of Leah—who in life thought she was unloved—that God blessed the world with our Savior. Jesus brings justice, restores hope, and gives us an inheritance beyond our wildest dreams.

MAKING IT WORK

Are there some things in your life that don't seem fair? How does the promise of "hope in the Lord" help you face them? Think about three ways God's love and salvation gives you hope when things don't seem to be going right.

_____

_____

_____

_____

_____

_____

_____

_____

_____

_____

_____

_____

_____

_____

_____

When the Water Blushed

JOHN 1:1–14

~~~~~~~~

In the beginning was the Word. . . .
Through him all things were made.

—JOHN 1:1, 3

Why did Jesus come to Earth before the invention of photography and video? Couldn't He have reached more people if everyone could see Him? After all, a picture is worth a thousand words.

Someone once turned that around and said that a word can be worth a thousand pictures. Consider poet Richard Crashaw's magnificent line about what happened when Jesus was asked to help out at a marriage in Cana, "The conscious water saw its Master and blushed." In one simple line, Crashaw captures the essence of Jesus's first miracle (John 2:1–11). Creation itself recognizes Jesus as the Creator. No mere carpenter could turn water to wine.

Another time, when Christ calmed a storm with the words, "Quiet! Be still," His stunned disciples asked, "Who is this? Even the wind and the waves obey him!" (Mark 4:39, 41). Later, Jesus told the Pharisees that if the crowd did not praise Him, "the stones will cry out" (Luke 19:40). Even the rocks know who He is.

John tells us, "The Word became flesh and made his dwelling among us. We have seen his glory" (John 1:14). Out of that eyewitness experience John also wrote, "We proclaim to you the one who existed from the beginning, whom we have heard and seen. . . . He is the Word of life" (1 John 1:1 NLT). Like John, we can use our words to introduce others to Jesus—the One the winds and water obey.

MAKING IT WORK

The plan for the gospel of Jesus to be made known has always been one believer telling someone else about the Savior. How can you be a part of that plan? Is there anyone in your life you feel you could share your faith story with as a way of introducing that person to Jesus?

_____

_____

_____

_____

_____

_____

_____

_____

_____

_____

_____

_____

_____

_____

_____

_____

_____

_____

Chili Peppers

JAMES 1:22–27

~~~~~~~~

Religion that God our Father accepts as pure and faultless is this: to look after orphans and widows in their distress.

—JAMES 1:27

"My mother gave us chili peppers before we went to bed," said Samuel, recalling his difficult childhood in sub-Saharan Africa. "We drank water to cool our mouths, and then we would feel full." He added, "It did not work well."

Government upheaval had forced Samuel's father to flee for his life, leaving their mother as the family's sole provider. Sam's brother had sickle cell anemia, and they couldn't afford medical care. Their mother took them to church, but it didn't mean much to Sam. *How could God allow our family to suffer like this?* he wondered.

Then one day a man learned about their plight and brought them some medicine to help with treatment. "On Sunday we will go to this man's church," his mother announced. Right away Sam sensed something different about this church. The people there celebrated their relationship with Jesus by living His love.

That was three decades ago. Today in his part of the world, Sam has started more than twenty churches, a large school, and a home for orphans. He's continuing the legacy of true religion taught by James, the brother of Jesus, who urged us not to "merely listen to the word" but to "do what it says" (James 1:22). "Religion that God our Father accepts as pure and faultless is this: to look after orphans and widows in their distress" (v. 27).

There's no telling what a simple act of kindness done in Jesus's name can do.

MAKING IT WORK

Think about how transforming a single benevolent act can be. We don't have to be famous or rich or influential. We just have to look for the small opportunities God gives us to serve and help others—and then do it. If we look at others with the eyes of caring, it won't be hard to find ways to help them.

The Death of Doubt

JOHN 11:1–16

---

*Unless I see the nail marks in his hands
and put my finger where the nails were, and put
my hand into his side, I will not believe.*

— JOHN 20:25

We know him as Doubting Thomas (see John 20:24–29), but the label isn't entirely fair. After all, how many of us would have believed that our executed leader had been resurrected? We might just as well call him "Courageous Thomas." The disciple known for his doubt displayed impressive courage as Jesus moved purposefully into the events leading to His death.

At the death of Lazarus, Jesus had said, "Let us go back to Judea" (John 11:7), prompting a protest from the disciples. "Rabbi," they said, "a short while ago the Jews there tried to stone you, and yet you are going back?" (v. 8). It was Thomas who said, "Let us also go, that we may die with him" (v. 16).

Thomas's intentions proved nobler than his actions. Upon Jesus's arrest, Thomas fled with the rest (Matthew 26:56), leaving Peter and John to accompany Christ to the courtyard of the high priest. Only John followed Jesus all the way to the cross.

Despite having witnessed the resurrection of Lazarus (John 11:38–44), Thomas still could not bring himself to believe that the crucified Lord had conquered death. Not until Thomas the doubter—the human—saw the risen Lord, could he exclaim, "My Lord and my God!" (John 20:28). Jesus's response gave assurance to the doubter and immeasurable comfort to us: "Because you have seen me, you have believed; blessed are those who have not seen and yet have believed" (v. 29).

MAKING IT WORK

We read about Thomas and his insistence on physical evidence, and we understand. But did you know that Jesus had a message for those of us who would believe without physical evidence? In addition to John 20:29, read John 17:20–21. That's us. How amazing is this?

_____

_____

_____

_____

_____

_____

_____

_____

_____

_____

_____

_____

_____

_____

_____

What's in a Name?

LUKE 3:31; 1 CHRONICLES 3:4–9

～～～～

[Jesus] was the son, so it was thought, of Joseph.

—LUKE 3:23

In God's timing, our son Kofi was born on a Friday, which is exactly what his name means—boy born on Friday. We named him after a Ghanaian friend of ours, a pastor whose only son died. He prays for our Kofi constantly. We're deeply honored.

It's easy to miss the significance in a name if you don't know the story behind it. In Luke 3, we find a fascinating detail about a name in the ancestry of Joseph. The genealogy traces Joseph's line backwards all the way to Adam and even to God (v. 38). In verse 31 we read: "the son of Nathan, the son of David." Nathan? That's interesting. In 1 Chronicles 3:5 we learn that Nathan was born to Bathsheba.

Is it coincidence that David named Bathsheba's child Nathan? Recall the backstory. Bathsheba was never supposed to be David's wife. Another Nathan—the prophet—bravely confronted the king for abusing his authority to exploit Bathsheba and murder her husband (see 2 Samuel 12).

David accepted the prophet's point-blank rebuke and repented of his horrific offenses. With the healing passage of time, he would name his son Nathan. How appropriate that this was Bathsheba's son, and that he would be one of the ancestors of Joseph, Jesus's earthly dad (Luke 3:23).

In the Bible, we keep finding God's grace woven into everything—even into an obscure name in a seldom-read genealogy. God's grace is everywhere.

MAKING IT WORK

Grace is not a word we hear a lot about in our world—especially the work world, which can be cutthroat. What are some ways to incorporate grace into your daily interactions with others? What about at home with the family?

_____

_____

_____

_____

_____

_____

_____

_____

_____

_____

_____

_____

_____

_____

_____

_____

_____

_____

An Open Hand

ACTS 20:22–35

～～～～～

It is more blessed to give than to receive.

—ACTS 20:35

In 1891, Biddy Mason was laid to rest in an unmarked grave in Los Angeles. That wasn't unusual for a woman born into slavery, but it was remarkable for someone as accomplished as Biddy. After winning her freedom in a court battle in 1856, she combined her nursing skills with wise business decisions to make a small fortune. As she observed the plight of immigrants and prisoners, she reached out to them, investing in charity so frequently that people began lining up at her house for help. In 1872, just sixteen years out of slavery, she and her son-in-law financed the founding of the First African Methodist Episcopal Church in Los Angeles.

Biddy embodied the apostle Paul's words: "I showed you that by this kind of hard work we must help the weak, remembering the words the Lord Jesus himself said: 'It is more blessed to give than to receive'" (Acts 20:35). Paul came from privilege, not slavery, yet he chose a life that would lead to his imprisonment and martyrdom so he could serve Christ and others.

In 1988, benefactors unveiled a tombstone for Biddy Mason. In attendance were the mayor of Los Angeles and nearly 3,000 members of the little church that had begun in her home over a century earlier. Biddy once said, "The open hand is blessed, for it gives in abundance even as it receives." The hand that gave so generously received a rich legacy.

MAKING IT WORK

What do you think it means to have an "open hand" in regard to others—especially those in need? What are a couple of ways you and your family could provide assistance to help those who can't help themselves? If you are a father, what legacy do you want to leave in regard to the poor of your community?

_____

_____

_____

_____

_____

_____

_____

_____

_____

_____

_____

_____

_____

_____

_____

_____

_____

_____

_____

All of Me

MATTHEW 27:45–54

~~~~~~~~

Offer your bodies as a living sacrifice, holy and pleasing
to God—this is your true and proper worship.

—ROMANS 12:1

Young Isaac Watts (1674–1748) found the music in his church sadly lacking, and his father challenged him to create something better. Isaac did. His hymn "When I Survey the Wondrous Cross" has been called the greatest in the English language and has been translated into many other languages.

Watts's worshipful third verse ushers us into the presence of Christ at the crucifixion.

> **See from His head, His hands, His feet,**
> **Sorrow and love flow mingled down.**
> **Did e'er such love and sorrow meet**
> **Or thorns compose so rich a crown?**

The crucifixion Watts describes so elegantly stands as history's most awful moment. We do well to pause and stand with those around the cross. The Son of God strains for breath, held by crude spikes driven through His flesh. After tortured hours, a supernatural darkness descends. Finally, mercifully, the Lord of the universe dismisses His anguished spirit. An earthquake rattles the landscape. Back in the city the thick temple curtain rips in half. Graves open, and dead bodies resurrect, walking about the city (Matthew 27:51–53). These events compel the centurion who crucified Jesus to say, "Surely he was the Son of God!" (v. 54).

"The Cross reorders all values and cancels all vanities," says the Poetry Foundation in commenting on Watts's poem. The song could only conclude: "Love so amazing, so divine demands my soul, my life, my all."

MAKING IT WORK

What song grabs your heart as "When I Survey" has touched believers for centuries? In what way does a singable tune move you toward God in a way nothing else can?

_____

_____

_____

_____

_____

_____

_____

_____

_____

_____

_____

_____

_____

_____

My Brothers and Sisters

MATTHEW 25:31–40

~~~~~~

Whatever you did for one of the least of these brothers and sisters of mine, you did for me.

—MATTHEW 25:40

Several years ago when the Southern California economy took a downturn, Pastor Bob Johnson saw not only difficulty but also opportunity. So he scheduled a meeting with the mayor of his city and asked, "What can our church do to help you?" The mayor was astonished. People usually came to him for help. Here was a minister offering him the services of an entire congregation.

Together the mayor and pastor came up with a plan to address several pressing needs. In their county alone, more than 20,000 seniors had gone the previous year without a single visitor. Hundreds of foster children needed families. And many other kids needed tutoring to help them succeed in school.

Some of those needs could be addressed without much financial investment, but they all required time and interest. And that's what the church had to give.

Jesus told His disciples about a future day in which He would say to His faithful followers, "Come, you who are blessed by my Father; take your inheritance" (Matthew 25:34). He also said they would express surprise at their reward. Then He would tell them, "Whatever you did for one of the least of these brothers and sisters of mine, you did for me" (v. 40).

God's kingdom work gets done when we give generously of the time, love, and resources He has provided us.

MAKING IT WORK

Who are some people you know who would fit into the "least of these" category? Do they know that you care for them? Would even a friendly conversation with them be an encouragement to them (and surprisingly to you too)? Is there something tangible you could do for them?

_____

_____

_____

_____

_____

_____

_____

_____

_____

_____

_____

_____

_____

_____

_____

_____

_____

_____

Skywatcher

ISAIAH 40:21–31

*He . . . brings out the starry host one by one
and calls forth each of them by name.*

—ISAIAH 40:26

Unsettled by issues at work and at home, Matt decided to take a walk. The evening spring air beckoned. As the infinite sky deepened from blue to black, a thickening fog spilled slowly over the marsh. Stars began to glimmer, heralding the full moon rising in the east. The moment, for Matt, was deeply spiritual. *He's there*, he thought. *God is there, and He's got this.*

Some people look at the night sky and see nothing but nature. Others see a god as distant and cold as Jupiter. But the same God who "sits enthroned above the circle of the earth" also "brings out the starry host one by one and calls forth each of them by name" (Isaiah 40:22, 26). He knows His creation intimately.

It is this personal God who asked His people, "Why do you say, Israel, 'My way is hidden from the Lord; my cause is disregarded by my God'?" Aching for them, God reminded them of the wisdom in seeking Him. "Do you not know? Have you not heard? . . . He gives strength to the weary and increases the power of the weak" (vv. 27–29).

We are easily tempted to forget God. Our problems won't disappear with an evening stroll, but we can find rest and certainty that God is always working toward His good purposes. "I'm here," He says. "I've got you."

MAKING IT WORK

Think of what God has created! Our universe is so massive and so exciting that we can't help but be in awe of its Creator. But think of it this way: If He is great enough to create all that, surely He is great enough to care for, protect, and love us—His favorite creatures. How might you praise Him in this moment?

_____

_____

_____

_____

_____

_____

_____

_____

_____

_____

_____

_____

_____

_____

_____

_____

_____

_____

_____

God's Hearts for Hypocrites

GENESIS 38:16–26

~~~~~

She is more righteous than I.

— GENESIS 38:26

"I'd be very disappointed if one of our team members did that," said a cricket player, referring to a South African cricketer who had cheated in a match. But only two years later, that same player was caught in a nearly identical scandal.

Few things rankle us more than hypocrisy. But in the story of Judah in Genesis 38, Judah's hypocritical behavior nearly had deadly consequences. After two of his sons died soon after marrying Tamar, Judah had quietly abandoned his duty to provide for her needs (vv. 8–11). In desperation, Tamar disguised herself by wearing a prostitute's veil, and Judah slept with her (vv. 15–16).

Yet when Judah learned that his widowed daughter-in-law was pregnant, his reaction was murderous. "Bring her out and have her burned to death!" he demanded (v. 24). But Tamar had proof that Judah was the father (v. 25).

Judah could have denied the truth. Instead he admitted his hypocrisy and also accepted his responsibility to care for her, saying, "She is more righteous than I" (v. 26).

And God wove even this dark chapter of Judah and Tamar's story into His story of our redemption. Tamar's children (vv. 29–30) would become ancestors of Jesus (Matthew 1:2–3).

Why is Genesis 38 in the Bible? One reason is because it's the story of our hypocritical human hearts—and of God's heart of love, grace, and mercy.

MAKING IT WORK

Hypocrisy in the church is one of the primary excuses our non-church friends use for staying away. Ask yourself this: "Is there anything I am doing that could contribute to that opinion of Christians?" And "What can I do to be more authentic in God's eyes and human opinion?"

The Money

MATTHEW 6:24–34

~~~~~~~

You cannot serve both God and money.

—MATTHEW 6:24

Early in my career, while doing work that I saw as more of a mission than a job, another company offered me a position that would give a significant increase in pay. Our family could surely have benefited financially from such a move. There was one problem. I hadn't been looking for another job. I loved my current role, which was growing into a calling.

But the money . . .

I called my father, then in his seventies, and explained the situation. Though his once-sharp mind had been slowed by strokes and the strain of years, his answer was crisp and clear: "Don't even think about the money. What would you do?"

In an instant, my mind was made up. The money would have been my only reason for leaving the job I loved! Thanks, Dad.

Jesus devoted a substantial section of His Sermon on the Mount to money and our fondness for it. He taught us to pray not for an accumulation of riches but for "our daily bread" (Matthew 6:11). He warned against storing up treasures on earth and pointed to the birds and flowers as evidence that God cares deeply about His creation (vv. 19–31). "Seek first his kingdom and his righteousness," Jesus said, "and all these things will be given to you as well" (v. 33).

Money matters. But money shouldn't rule our decision-making process. Tough times and big decisions are opportunities to grow our faith in new ways. Our heavenly Father cares for us.

MAKING IT WORK

How much of your time is spent thinking about and worrying about money? Do you need to consult someone who could give you good advice about money management? How can the problems and worries about money be turned into another way to trust and depend on God?

_____

_____

_____

_____

_____

_____

_____

_____

_____

_____

_____

_____

_____

_____

_____

_____

What's the Occasion?

ECCLESIASTES 3:9–17

~~~~~~~~

Everything God does will endure forever.

— ECCLESIASTES 3:14

Four-year-old Asher's gleeful face peeked out from beneath his favorite hooded sweatshirt—his alligator-head hooded sweatshirt complete with plush jaws that seemed to swallow his head! His mom's heart sank. She wanted the family to make a good impression as they visited a family they hadn't seen in a long time.

"Oh, Son," she said, "that may not be appropriate for the occasion."

"Of course it is!" Asher protested brightly.

"Hmm, and what occasion might that be?" she asked. Asher replied, "You know. Life!" He got to wear the shirt.

That joyful boy already grasps the truth of Ecclesiastes 3:12: "There is nothing better for people than to be happy and to do good while they live." Ecclesiastes can seem depressing and is often misunderstood because it's written from a human perspective, not God's. The writer, King Solomon, asked, "What do workers gain from their toil?" (v. 9). Yet throughout the book we catch glimpses of hope. Solomon also wrote: "That each of [us] may eat and drink, and find satisfaction in all [our] toil—this is the gift of God" (v. 13).

We serve a God who gives us good things to enjoy. Everything He does "will endure forever" (v. 14). As we acknowledge Him and follow His loving commands, He infuses our lives with purpose, meaning, and joy.

MAKING IT WORK

Life! How is it going for you? What do you feel your purpose is in life? What gives life meaning for you? Where do you find joy? How does God interact with those answers?

_____

_____

_____

_____

_____

_____

_____

_____

_____

_____

_____

_____

_____

_____

_____

_____

_____

_____

_____

_____

Not a Simple Story

2 CHRONICLES 16:7–14

〰〰〰

*The eyes of the LORD range throughout the earth to
strengthen those whose hearts are fully committed to him.*

— 2 CHRONICLES 16:9

Life seems straightforward in the laws of the Old Testament. Obey God and get blessed. Disobey Him and expect trouble. It's a satisfying theology. But is it that simple?

King Asa's story seems to fit the pattern. He led his people away from false gods, and his kingdom thrived (2 Chronicles 15:1–19). Then, late in his reign, he depended on himself instead of God (16:2–7). The rest of his life was marked by war and illness (v. 12).

It's easy to look at that story and draw a simple conclusion. But when the prophet Hanani warned Asa, he said that God will "strengthen those whose hearts are fully committed to him" (16:9). Why do our hearts need strengthening? Because doing the right thing may require courage and perseverance.

Job got the starring role in a cosmic tragedy. His crime? "He [was] blameless and upright" (Job 1:8). Joseph, falsely accused of attempted rape, languished in prison for years—to serve God's good purposes (Genesis 39:19–41:1). And Jeremiah was beaten and put in stocks (Jeremiah 20:2). What was the prophet's offense? Telling the truth to rebellious people (26:15).

Life is not simple, and God's ways are not our ways. Making the right decision may come at a cost. But in God's eternal plan, His blessings arrive in due time.

MAKING IT WORK

What were a couple of situations when you were wrongly accused and had to pay unfair consequences? What did that teach you about life in a fallen world? Were you still able to continue to trust God? What does Joseph's story teach in that regard?

_____

_____

_____

_____

_____

_____

_____

_____

_____

_____

_____

_____

_____

_____

_____

_____

_____

_____

Little Lies and Kittens

ROMANS 5:12–21

~~~~~~~

*Just as sin ruled over all people and brought them to
death, now God's wonderful grace rules instead.*

— ROMANS 5:21 NLT

Mom noticed four-year-old Elias as he scurried away from the
newborn kittens. She had told him not to touch them. "Did you
touch the kitties, Elias?" she asked.

"No!" he said earnestly. So Mom had another question: "Were
they soft?"

"Yes," he volunteered, "and the black one mewed."

With a toddler, we smile at such duplicity. But Elias's disobe-
dience underscores our human condition. No one has to teach
a four-year-old to lie. "For I was born a sinner," wrote David in
his classic confession, "yes, from the moment my mother conceived me" (Psalm 51:5 NLT). The apostle Paul said: "When Adam
sinned, sin entered the world. Adam's sin brought death, so death
spread to everyone, for everyone sinned" (Romans 5:12 NLT). That
depressing news applies equally to kings, four-year-olds, and you
and me.

But there's plenty of hope! "God's law was given so that all
people could see how sinful they were," wrote Paul. "But as peo-

ple sinned more and more, God's wonderful grace became more abundant" (Romans 5:20 NLT).

God is not waiting for us to blow it so He can pounce on us. He is the author of grace, forgiveness, and restoration. We need to recognize that our sin is neither cute nor excusable and then come to Him in faith and repentance.

MAKING IT WORK

What does grace mean to you? Think about how you have shown grace to your children or your wife. It feels great to show grace, doesn't it? God loves to be gracious to us. Do you need to have God's grace work for you in some area of life?

_____

_____

_____

_____

_____

_____

_____

_____

_____

_____

_____

_____

_____

_____

_____

_____

_____

_____

Words That Matter

1 JOHN 1:1–4

~~~~~~

That which was from the beginning, which we have heard, which we have seen with our eyes . . . this we proclaim concerning the Word of life.

— 1 JOHN 1:1

Early in my days of working as an editor for *Our Daily Bread*, I selected the verse that appeared on the cover of each month's devotional. After a while, I began to wonder if it made a difference.

Not long after that, a reader wrote and described how she had prayed for her son for more than twenty years, yet he wanted nothing to do with Jesus. Then one day he stopped by to visit her, and he read the verse on the cover of the copy of *Our Daily Bread* that sat on her table. The Spirit used those words to convict him, and he gave his life to Jesus at that very moment.

I don't recall the verse or the woman's name. But I'll never forget the clarity of God's message to me that day. He had chosen to answer a woman's prayers through a verse selected nearly a year earlier. From a place beyond time, He brought the wonder of His presence to my work and His words.

John the disciple called Jesus "the Word of life" (1 John 1:1). He wanted everyone to know what that meant. "We proclaim to you the eternal life, which was with the Father and has appeared to us," he wrote of Jesus (v. 2). "We proclaim to you what we have seen and heard, so that you also may have fellowship with us" (v. 3).

There is nothing magical in putting words on a page. But there is life-changing power in the words of Scripture because they point us to the Word of life—Jesus.

MAKING IT WORK

As you think through "the words of Scripture," what are two or three passages that give you the most guidance or encouragement or challenge? Would it be good to memorize those words and study them in depth in their context?

_____

_____

_____

_____

_____

_____

_____

_____

_____

_____

_____

_____

_____

_____

_____

_____

_____

_____

Kossi's Courage

2 KINGS 23:12–14, 21–25

~~~~~~

You shall have no other gods before me. . . .
You shall not bow down to them or worship them.

—EXODUS 20:3, 5

As he awaited his baptism in Togo's Mono River, Kossi stooped to pick up a worn wooden carving. His family had worshiped the object for generations. Now they watched as he tossed the grotesque figure into a fire prepared for the occasion. No longer would their choicest chickens be sacrificed to this god.

In the West, most Christians think of idols as metaphors for what they put in place of God. In Togo, West Africa, idols represent literal gods that must be appeased with sacrifice. Idol burning and baptism make a courageous statement about a new believer's allegiance to the one true God.

As an eight-year-old, King Josiah came to power in an idol-worshiping, sex-obsessed culture. His father and grandfather had been two of the worst kings in all of Judah's sordid history. Then the high priest discovered the book of the law. When the young king heard its words, he took them to heart (2 Kings 22:8–13). Josiah destroyed the pagan altars, burned the vile items dedicated to the goddess Asherah, and stopped the ritual prostitution (chapter 23). In place of these practices, he celebrated the Passover (23:21–23).

Whenever we look for answers apart from God—consciously or subconsciously—we pursue a false god. It would be wise to ask ourselves: What idols, literal or figurative, do we need to throw on the fire?

MAKING IT WORK

In much of the twenty-first century world, this concept of having idols might be a tough one to understand. Yet anything we treat as more important than God can be seen that way. We need to see if there is anything approaching that importance in our lives.

_____

_____

_____

_____

_____

_____

_____

_____

_____

_____

_____

_____

_____

_____

_____

_____

_____

_____

The Gift of Giving

LUKE 3:7–14

~~~~~~~~

Each of you should give what you have decided in your heart to give, not reluctantly or under compulsion.

—2 CORINTHIANS 9:7

A pastor breathed life into the phrase "He'd give you the shirt off his back" when he gave this unsettling challenge to his church: "What would happen if we took the coats off our backs and gave them to the needy?" Then he took his own coat and laid it at the front of the church. Dozens of others followed his example. This was during the winter, so the trip home was less comfortable that day. But for dozens of people in need, the season warmed up just a bit.

When John the Baptist roamed the Judean wilderness, he had a stern warning for the crowd that came to hear him. "You brood of vipers!" he said. "Produce fruit in keeping with repentance" (Luke 3:7–8). Startled, they asked him, "What should we do then?" He responded with this advice: "Anyone who has two shirts should share with the one who has none, and anyone who has food should do the same" (vv. 10–11). True repentance produces a generous heart.

Because "God loves a person who gives cheerfully" (NLT), giving should never be guilt-based or pressured (2 Corinthians 9:7).

But when we give freely and generously, we find that it truly is more blessed to give than to receive.

MAKING IT WORK

Can you think of a time when you gave a gift to someone but gave it grudgingly? How did that feel? Now think of a time when you gave out of love, compassion, or the joy of giving. It's not surprising that we feel a difference in those two situations. How can this guide us in our giving?

_____

_____

_____

_____

_____

_____

_____

_____

_____

_____

_____

_____

_____

_____

_____

_____

_____

_____

_____

_____

_____

What on Earth?

MATTHEW 17:24–27

~~~~~~~~

*My God will meet all your needs according
to the riches of his glory in Christ Jesus.*

— PHILIPPIANS 4:19

When Andrew Cheatle lost his cell phone at the beach, he thought it was gone forever. About a week later, however, fisherman Glen Kerley called him. He had pulled Cheatle's phone, still functional after it dried, out of a twenty-five-pound cod.

Life is full of odd stories, and we find more than a few of them in the Bible. One day tax collectors came to Peter demanding to know, "Doesn't your teacher pay the temple tax?" (Matthew 17:24). Jesus turned the situation into a teaching moment. He wanted Peter to understand His role as king. Taxes weren't collected from the children of the king, and the Lord made it clear that neither He nor His children owed any temple tax (vv. 25–26).

Yet Jesus wanted to be careful not to "cause offense" (v. 27), so He told Peter to go fishing. (This is the odd part of the story.) Peter found a coin in the mouth of the first fish he caught.

What on earth is Jesus doing here? A better question is, "What in God's kingdom is Jesus doing?" He is the rightful

King—even when many do not recognize Him as such. When we accept His role as Lord in our lives, we become His children.

Life will still throw its various demands at us, but Jesus will provide for us. As Pastor David Pompo put it, "When we're fishing for our Father, we can depend on Him for all we need."

MAKING IT WORK

What odd or surprising things has God done in your life? What have you learned about Him through His uncommon interactions with you?

_____

_____

_____

_____

_____

_____

_____

_____

_____

_____

_____

_____

_____

_____

_____

_____

_____

_____

_____

_____

_____

Just a Touch

MATTHEW 8:1–16

～～～

Jesus reached out his hand and touched the man.

—MATTHEW 8:3

Kiley leaped at the chance to go to a remote area of East Africa to assist a medical mission, yet she felt uneasy. She didn't have any medical experience. Still, she could provide basic care.

While there, she met a woman with a horrible but treatable disease. The woman's distorted leg repulsed her, but Kiley knew she had to do something. As she cleaned and bandaged the leg, her patient began crying. Concerned, Kiley asked if she was hurting her. "No," she replied. "It's the first time in nine years that anyone has touched me."

Leprosy is another disease that can render its victims repulsive to others, and ancient Jewish culture had strict guidelines to prevent its spread: "They must live alone," the law declared about lepers. "They must live outside the camp" (Leviticus 13:46).

That's why it's so remarkable that a leper approached Jesus to say, "Lord, if you are willing, you can make me clean" (Matthew 8:2). "Jesus reached out his hand and touched the man. 'I am willing,' he said. 'Be clean!'" (v. 3).

In touching a lonely woman's diseased leg, Kiley began to show the fearless, bridge-building love of Jesus. A single touch made a difference.

MAKING IT WORK

What challenging ministry of helping someone else would you do if you could overcome the fear of the challenge? Working with a different culture than your own? Working with young people? Providing assistance to some struggling men in your church? How can you start to reach out like Jesus?

_____

_____

_____

_____

_____

_____

_____

_____

_____

_____

_____

_____

_____

_____

_____

_____

_____

_____

_____

Desperate Solutions

ISAIAH 22:8–13

*You did not . . . have regard for
the One who planned it long ago.*

—ISAIAH 22:11

In the late sixteenth century, William of Orange intentionally flooded much of the Netherlands. The Dutch monarch resorted to such a drastic measure in an attempt to drive out the invading Spaniards. It didn't work, and a vast swath of prime farmland was lost to the sea. "Desperate times call for desperate measures," they say.

In Isaiah's day, Jerusalem turned to desperate measures when the Assyrian army threatened them. Creating a water storage system to endure the siege, the people also tore down houses to shore up the city walls. Such tactics may have been prudent, but they neglected the most important step. "You built a reservoir between the two walls for the water of the Old Pool," God said, "but you did not look to the One who made it, or have regard for the One who planned it long ago" (Isaiah 22:11).

We aren't likely to encounter a literal army outside our homes today. "The batterings always come in commonplace ways and through commonplace people," said Oswald Chambers. Yet, such "batterings" are genuine threats. Thankfully, they also bring with them God's invitation to turn to Him first for what we need.

When life's irritations and interruptions come, will we see them as opportunities to turn to God? Or will we seek our own desperate solutions?

MAKING IT WORK

What challenge came into your life that was turned into a great opportunity or a great victory? Sometimes God works that way. Try it today. When faced with a situation that seems daunting, see how you can turn it into a God-directed victory.

_____

_____

_____

_____

_____

_____

_____

_____

_____

_____

_____

_____

_____

_____

_____

_____

_____

_____

_____

_____

~~~~~

"When life's irritations
and interruptions come,
will we see them as
opportunities to turn to God?"

~~~~~

Silence

HABAKKUK 1:1–4; 2:20

~~~~~~

How long, LORD, must I call for help,
but you do not listen?

— HABAKKUK 1:2

Skittish chickens scattered as relief trucks clattered past the weathered huts of the village. Barefoot children stared. Traffic on this rain-ravaged "road" was rare.

Suddenly, a walled mansion loomed into view of the convoy. It was the mayor's house—although he didn't live in it. His people lacked basic necessities, while he lounged in luxury in a distant city.

Such unfairness angers us. It angered God's prophet too. When Habakkuk saw rampant oppression he asked, "How long, LORD, must I call for help, but you do not listen?" (Habakkuk 1:2). But God had noticed, and He said, "Woe to him who piles up stolen goods . . . who builds his house by unjust gain!" (2:6, 9). Judgment was coming!

We welcome God's judgment of others, but there's a pivot point in Habakkuk that gives us pause: "The LORD is in his holy temple; let all the earth be silent before him" (2:20). *All* the earth. The oppressed along with oppressors. Sometimes the appropriate response to God's seeming silence is . . . silence!

Why silence? Because we easily overlook our own spiritual poverty. Silence allows us to recognize our sinfulness in the presence of a holy God.

Habakkuk learned to trust God, and we can too. We don't know all His ways, but we do know that He is good. Nothing is beyond His control and timing.

MAKING IT WORK

Spiritual retreats may sound like a good idea, but who has time or wherewithal to go for a long weekend with nobody around but God? So, we have to create our own times—even if they are just a few minutes—to get alone with God. Can you see yourself doing that and listening for God to speak to you through the Spirit and God's Word?

_____

_____

_____

_____

_____

_____

_____

_____

_____

_____

_____

_____

_____

_____

_____

_____

Signs and Feelings

MATTHEW 16:1–4

~~~~~~~

Your word is a lamp for my feet, a light on my path.

— PSALM 119:105

A young man I know has a habit of asking God for signs. That's not necessarily bad, but his prayers tend to seek confirmation of his feelings. For instance, he'll pray, "God, if You want me to do X, then You please do Y, and I'll know it's okay."

This has created a dilemma. Because of the way he prays and the way he thinks God is answering, he feels that he should get back with his ex-girlfriend. Perhaps unsurprisingly, she feels strongly that God doesn't want that.

The religious leaders of Jesus's day demanded a sign from Him to prove the validity of His claims (Matthew 16:1). They weren't seeking God's guidance; they were challenging His divine authority. Jesus replied, "A wicked and adulterous generation looks for a sign" (v. 4). The Lord's strong response wasn't a blanket statement to prevent anyone from seeking God's guidance. Rather, Jesus was accusing them of ignoring the clear prophecies in Scripture that indicated He was the Messiah.

God wants us to seek His guidance in prayer (James 1:5). He also gives us the guidance of the Spirit (John 14:26) and

His Word (Psalm 119:105). He provides us with mentors and wise leaders. And He's given us the example of Jesus himself.

MAKING IT WORK

Think of the toolbox of spiritual tools God has provided for us: prayer, the Holy Spirit, the Bible, Christian friends, pastors and teachers. You'd need a Craftsman five-drawer toolbox to organize it all! Which of these tools seem to be unused and neglected? Which should you take out of the drawer and put to work?

_____

_____

_____

_____

_____

_____

_____

_____

_____

_____

_____

_____

_____

_____

_____

_____

_____

_____

_____

_____

Getting Away with It

GENESIS 4:1–12

~~~~~~~~

By faith Abel still speaks.

— HEBREWS 11:4

In June 2004, at a Vancouver art gallery, Canadian cross-country skier Beckie Scott received an Olympic gold medal. That's interesting, because the Winter Olympics had been held in 2002—in Utah. Scott had won bronze behind two athletes who were disqualified months later when it was learned they had used banned substances.

It's good that Scott eventually received her gold, but gone forever is the moment when she should have stood on the podium to hear her country's national anthem. That injustice couldn't be remedied.

Injustice of any kind disturbs us, and surely there are far greater wrongs than being denied a hard-won medal. The story of Cain and Abel shows an ultimate act of injustice (Genesis 4:8). And at first glance, it might look like Cain got away with murdering his brother. After all, he lived a long, full life, eventually building a city (v. 17).

But God himself confronted Cain. "Your brother's blood cries out to me from the ground," He said (v. 10). The New Testament later recorded Cain as an example to avoid (1 John 3:12; Jude 1:11). But of Abel we read, "By faith Abel still speaks, even though he is dead" (Hebrews 11:4).

God cares deeply about justice, about righting wrongs, and about defending the powerless. In the end, no one gets away with any act of injustice. Nor does God leave unrewarded our work done in faith for Him.

MAKING IT WORK

The fact that past injustices of all kinds cannot be undone should alert us to the goal of stopping unfair treatment of others whenever we can. Do you see any such activities happening in your world—situations where you could change someone's life by making sure someone is treated properly as a person made in God's image?

_____

_____

_____

_____

_____

_____

_____

_____

_____

_____

_____

_____

_____

_____

_____

_____

_____

Not What It Seems

2 KINGS 19:29–37

~~~~~~~~~~

Do not believe every spirit, but test the spirits
to see whether they are from God.

— 1 JOHN 4:1

"Listen!" my wife said to me over the phone. "There's a monkey in our yard!" She held up the phone so I could hear. And yes, it sounded just like a monkey. Which is weird, because the nearest wild monkey was 2,000 miles away.

Later, my father-in-law burst our bubble. "That's a barred owl," he explained. Reality was not what it had seemed.

When King Sennacherib's armies had Judah's King Hezekiah trapped inside Jerusalem's walls, the Assyrians thought victory was theirs. Reality proved different. Although the Assyrian field commander used smooth words and pretended to speak for God, the Lord had His hand on His people.

"Have I come to attack and destroy this place without word from the LORD?" the commander asked (2 Kings 18:25). As he tried to entice Jerusalem to surrender, he even said, "Choose life and not death!" (v. 32).

That sounds like something God would say. But the prophet Isaiah told the Israelites the true words of the Lord. "[Sennacherib] will not enter this city or shoot an arrow here," God said. "I will defend this city and save it" (19:32–34; Isaiah 37:35). That very night "the angel of the LORD" destroyed the Assyrians (v. 35).

From time to time, we'll encounter smooth-talking people who "advise" us while denying God's power. That isn't God's voice. He speaks to us through His Word. He guides us with His Spirit. His hand is on those who follow Him, and He will never abandon us.

MAKING IT WORK

We have to be careful who we listen to regarding how God works. What filters do you use to make sure advice is godly? We have to be careful because God's Word can be easily twisted to say what we want it to say.

_____

_____

_____

_____

_____

_____

_____

_____

_____

_____

_____

_____

_____

_____

_____

_____

Forged in Crisis

PSALM 57

~~~~~~~~~

I will take refuge in the shadow of your wings
until the disaster has passed.

— PSALM 57:1

Marc recalls a moment from his childhood when his father called the family together. Their car had broken down, and the family would run out of money by the end of the month. Marc's dad paused and prayed. Then he asked the family to expect God's answer.

Today Marc recalls how God's help arrived in surprising ways. A friend repaired their car; unexpected checks arrived; food showed up at the door. Praising God came easily. But the family's gratitude had been forged in a crisis.

Psalm 57 has long provided rich inspiration for worship songs. When David declared, "Be exalted, O God, above the heavens" (v. 11), we might imagine him gazing up at a magnificent Middle Eastern night sky or perhaps singing in a tabernacle worship service. But in reality David, fearful for his life, was hiding in a cave.

"I am in the midst of lions," David said in the psalm. These "ravenous beasts" were "men whose teeth are spears and arrows, whose tongues are sharp swords" (v. 4). David's praise was conceived in crisis. Although he was cornered by enemies who wanted him dead, David could write these amazing words: "My heart, O God, is steadfast . . . . I will sing and make music" (v. 7).

Whatever crisis we face today, we can run to God for help. Then we can praise Him as we wait expectantly, confident in His infinitely creative care for us.

MAKING IT WORK

You're at your job and the tools you need (whether it's a computer, a chain saw, or an air compressor) fail. Or you can't seem to make the boss happy, no matter how hard you try. Can you still say, "My heart, O God, is steadfast . . . I will sing and make music"? Can you still praise God in the crisis, big or small? That's a huge challenge for all of us.

_____

_____

_____

_____

_____

_____

_____

_____

_____

_____

_____

_____

_____

_____

_____

_____

Powerful Baby

PSALM 13

~~~~~~~~

How long, LORD? Will you forget me forever? . . .
But I trust in your unfailing love.

— PSALM 13:1, 5

The first time I saw him, I cried. He looked like a perfect newborn asleep in his crib. But we knew he would never wake up. Not until he was in the arms of Jesus.

He clung to life for several months. Then his mother told us of his death in a heart-wrenching email. She wrote of "that deep, deep pain that groans inside you." Then she said, "How deeply God carved His work of love into our hearts through that little life! What a powerful life it was!"

Powerful? How could she say that?

This family's precious little boy showed them—and us—that we must depend on God for everything. Especially when things go horribly wrong! The hard yet comforting truth is that God meets us in our pain. He knows the grief of losing a Son.

In our deepest pain, we turn to the songs of David because he writes out of his own grief. "How long must I wrestle with my thoughts and day after day have sorrow in my heart?" he asked (Psalm 13:2). "Give light to my eyes, or I will sleep in death" (v. 3).

Yet David could give his biggest questions to God. "But I trust in your unfailing love; my heart rejoices in your salvation" (v. 5).

Only God can bring ultimate significance to our most tragic events.

MAKING IT WORK

Perhaps you've suffered a tragedy closer to you than the one in the story—maybe in your own family. You might be living in David's question: "How long must I . . . day after day have sorrow in my heart?" The key to returning to some hope of joy is to "trust in [God's] unfailing love." As hard as it sounds, seek ways to return to trust in the God who made you and saved you—and His wisdom—superintends all things.

_____

_____

_____

_____

_____

_____

_____

_____

_____

_____

_____

_____

_____

_____

_____

_____

Defending God

LUKE 9:51–56

～～～

A gentle answer turns away wrath,
but a harsh word stirs up anger.

—PROVERBS 15:1

The anti-God bumper stickers covering the car seized the attention of a university professor. As a former atheist himself, the professor thought perhaps the owner wanted to make believers angry. "The anger helps the atheist to justify his atheism," he explained. Then he warned, "All too often, the atheist gets exactly what he is looking for."

In recalling his own journey to faith, this professor noted the concern of a Christian friend who invited him to consider the truth of Christ. His friend's "sense of urgency was conveyed without a trace of anger." He never forgot the genuine respect and grace he received that day.

Believers in Jesus often take offense when others reject Him. But how does He feel about that rejection? Jesus constantly faced threats and hatred, yet He never took anyone's doubt about His deity personally. Once, when a village refused Him hospitality, James and John wanted instant retaliation. "Lord," they asked, "do you want us to call fire down from heaven to destroy them?"

(Luke 9:54). Jesus didn't want that, and He "turned and rebuked them" (v. 55). After all, "God did not send his Son into the world to condemn the world, but to save the world through him" (John 3:17).

It may surprise us to consider that God doesn't need us to defend Him. He wants us to *represent* Him! That takes time, work, restraint, and love.

MAKING IT WORK

Bumper stickers? Facebook memes? Bracelets? What is the best way to represent Christ to others? There are dozens of ways, but if we don't show love and godliness, who will pay attention? What method fits best with the skills and personality God has given you?

_____

_____

_____

_____

_____

_____

_____

_____

_____

_____

_____

_____

_____

_____

_____

_____

_____

What Do the Experts Say?

JOHN 5:31–40

~~~~~~

These are the very Scriptures that testify about me,
yet you refuse to come to me to have life.

—JOHN 5:39–40

Boston Globe columnist Jeff Jacoby writes of the "uncanny ability of experts to get things hopelessly, cataclysmically wrong." A quick glance at recent history shows he's right. The great inventor Thomas Edison, for instance, once declared that talking movies would never replace silent films. And in 1928, Henry Ford speculated, "People are becoming too intelligent ever to have another war." Countless other predictions by "experts" have missed the mark badly. Genius obviously has its limits.

Only one Person is completely reliable, and He had strong words for some so-called experts. The religious leaders of Jesus's day claimed to have the truth. These scholars and theologians thought they knew what the promised Messiah would be like when He arrived.

Jesus cautioned them, "You study the Scriptures diligently because you think that in them you have eternal life." Then He pointed out how they were missing the heart of the matter.

"These are the very Scriptures that testify about me, yet you refuse to come to me to have life" (John 5:39–40).

People will continue to make predictions, and they will range from the terrifying to the wildly optimistic. Many of them will be stated with a great deal of confidence and authority. Don't be alarmed. Our confidence remains in the One at the very heart of the Scriptures. He has a firm grip on us and on our future.

MAKING IT WORK

Just for fun: What prediction have you heard recently that seems outrageously improbable? What worries you about the future? Is it things you have no control over? Or things you can either change or simply entrust to an all-wise, omniscient God?

_____

_____

_____

_____

_____

_____

_____

_____

_____

_____

_____

_____

_____

_____

_____

_____

_____

Don't Walk Away

JEREMIAH 1:4–9

~~~~~~~~~

Before you were born I set you apart.

—JEREMIAH 1:5

In 1986, John Piper nearly quit as minister of a large church. At that time he admitted in his journal: "I am so discouraged. I am so blank. I feel like there are opponents on every hand." But Piper didn't walk away, and God used him to lead a thriving ministry that would eventually reach far beyond his church.

Although *success* is a word easily misunderstood, we might call John Piper successful. But what if his ministry had never flourished?

God gave the prophet Jeremiah a direct call. "Before I formed you in the womb I knew you," God said. "Before you were born I set you apart" (Jeremiah 1:5). God encouraged him not to fear his enemies, "for I am with you and will rescue you" (v. 8).

Jeremiah later lamented his commission with ironic language for a man with a prenatal calling. "Alas, my mother, that you gave me birth, a man with whom the whole land strives and contends!" (15:10).

God did protect Jeremiah, but his ministry never thrived. His people never repented. He saw them slaughtered, enslaved, and scattered. Yet despite a lifetime of discouragement and rejection, he never walked away. He knew that God didn't call him to success but to faithfulness. He trusted the God who called him. Jeremiah's resilient compassion shows us the heart of the Father, who yearns for everyone to turn to Him.

MAKING IT WORK

How will you know if you are a success? In what ways does our success matter to others? How does God view us in relation to success?

_____

_____

_____

_____

_____

_____

_____

_____

_____

_____

_____

_____

_____

_____

_____

_____

_____

_____

_____

_____

_____

_____

_____

Blooming in the Right Spot

1 SAMUEL 20:30–34

~~~~~~

So Jonathan made a covenant with the house of David.

— 1 SAMUEL 20:16

"A weed is any plant that grows where you don't want it," my father said, handing me the hoe. I wanted to leave the corn plant that had "volunteered" among the peas. But Dad, who had grown up on a farm, instructed me to pull it out. That lone cornstalk would do nothing but choke the peas and rob them of nutrients.

Human beings aren't plants—we have minds of our own and God-given free will. But sometimes we try to bloom where God doesn't intend us to be.

King Saul's son, the warrior-prince Jonathan, could have done that. He had every reason to expect to be king. But he saw God's blessing on David, and he recognized the envy and pride of his own father (1 Samuel 18:12–15). So rather than grasping for a throne that would never be his, Jonathan became David's closest friend, even saving his life (19:1–6; 20:1–4).

Some would say that Jonathan gave up too much. But how would we prefer to be remembered? Like the ambitious Saul, who clung to his kingdom and lost it? Or like Jonathan, who protected the life of a man who would become an honored ancestor of Jesus?

God's plan is always better than our own. We can fight against it and resemble a misplaced weed. Or we can accept His direction and become flourishing, fruitful plants in His garden. He leaves the choice with us.

MAKING IT WORK

Do you feel that you are where you should be in life? Sometimes God directs us to move on to a different situation; sometimes He wants us to thrive and flourish where we are. What factors would help you know which is your situation?

_____

_____

_____

_____

_____

_____

_____

_____

_____

_____

_____

_____

_____

_____

_____

_____

_____

_____

_____

_____

_____

Judging Origins

JUDGES 11:1–8, 29

~~~~~~~~~~

The Spirit of the LORD came on Jephthah.

—JUDGES 11:29

"Where are you from?" We often use that question to get to know someone better. But for many of us, the answer is complicated. Sometimes we don't want to share all the details.

In the book of Judges, Jephthah might not have wanted to answer that question at all. His half-brothers had chased him out of his hometown of Gilead for his "questionable" origins. "You are the son of another woman," they declared (Judges 11:2). The text says starkly, "His mother was a prostitute" (v. 1).

But Jephthah was a natural leader, and when a hostile tribe picked a fight with Gilead, the people who had sent him packing suddenly wanted him back. "Be our commander," they said (v. 6). Jephthah asked, "Didn't you hate me and drive me from my father's house?" (v. 7). After getting assurances that things would be different this time, he agreed to lead them. The Scripture tells us, "Then the Spirit of the LORD came on Jephthah" (v. 29). Through faith, he led them to a great victory. The New Testament mentions him in its list of heroes of the faith (Hebrews 11:32).

God often seems to choose the unlikeliest people to do His work, doesn't He? It doesn't matter where we're from, how we got here, or what we've done. What matters is that we respond in faith to His love.

MAKING IT WORK

Who are some unlikely people you know who are doing great things? Sometimes, for example, the guys in high school who seemed so unlikely to make something of themselves find the right niche and thrive. Perhaps there is an area you feel inadequate to tackle because of your background. Let God lead you to do unlikely things for Him.

_____

_____

_____

_____

_____

_____

_____

_____

_____

_____

_____

_____

_____

_____

_____

_____

_____

_____

The Professor's Confession

1 JOHN 3:11–18

~~~~~~~~~

This is how we know what love is:
Jesus Christ laid down his life for us.

— 1 JOHN 3:16

Horrified by his students' poor writing habits, renowned author and college professor David Foster Wallace (1962–2008) considered how he might improve their skills. That's when a startling question confronted him. The professor had to ask himself why a student would listen to someone "as smug, narrow, self-righteous, [and] condescending" as he was. He knew he had a problem with pride.

That professor could and did change, but he could never become one of his students. Yet when Jesus came to Earth, He showed us what humility looks like by becoming one of us. Stepping across all kinds of boundaries, Jesus made himself at home everywhere by serving, teaching, and doing the will of His Father.

Even as He was being crucified, Jesus prayed for forgiveness for His executioners (Luke 23:34). Straining for every anguished breath, He still granted eternal life to a criminal dying with Him (vv. 42–43).

Why would Jesus do that? Why would He serve people like us to the very end? The apostle John gets to the point. Out of love! He writes, "This is how we know what love is: Jesus Christ laid down his life for us." Then he drives that point home. "And we ought to lay down our lives for our brothers and sisters" (1 John 3:16).

Jesus showed us that His love eradicates our pride, our smugness, our condescension. And He did it in the most powerful way possible. He gave His life.

MAKING IT WORK

Is there any context in which people think you are proud or smug or condescending? That's not the Jesus way. What small changes in your conversations with others or your actions toward them can say, "You are important, and as a redeemed man for whom Jesus died, I'm here to serve you"?

_____

_____

_____

_____

_____

_____

_____

_____

_____

_____

_____

_____

_____

_____

_____

_____

_____

The Last Call

2 SAMUEL 1:17–27

~~~~~~~

How the mighty have fallen!

—2 SAMUEL 1:27

After serving his country for two decades as a helicopter pilot, James returned home to serve his community as a teacher. But he missed helicopters, so he took a job flying medical evacuations for a local hospital. He flew until late in his life.

Now it was time to say goodbye to him. As friends, family, and uniformed co-workers stood vigil at the cemetery, a colleague called in one last mission over the radio. Soon the distinctive sound of rotors beating the air could be heard. A helicopter circled over the memorial garden, hovered briefly to pay its respects, then headed back to the hospital. Not even the military personnel who were present could hold back the tears.

When King Saul and his son Jonathan were killed in battle, David wrote an elegy for the ages called "the lament of the bow" (2 Samuel 1:18). "A gazelle lies slain on your heights," he sang. "How the mighty have fallen!" (v. 19). Jonathan was David's closest friend and brother-in-arms. And although David and Saul had been enemies, David honored them both. "Weep for Saul," he wrote. "I grieve for you, Jonathan my brother" (vv. 24, 26).

Even the best goodbyes are oh-so-difficult. But for those who trust in the Lord, the memory is much more sweet than bitter, for it is never forever. How good it is when we can honor those who have served others!

MAKING IT WORK

Think of someone you knew who has died—but who lived for Jesus. What are two great examples from that person's life that you can apply to how you live? Applying such things to our lives helps that person's godly legacy live on.

_____

_____

_____

_____

_____

_____

_____

_____

_____

_____

_____

_____

_____

_____

_____

_____

_____

_____

_____

_____

And in Truth

ZEPHANIAH 1:1–6; 2:1–3

~~~~~~

In his love he will no longer rebuke you,
but will rejoice over you with singing.

—ZEPHANIAH 3:17

Years ago, I attended a wedding where two people from different countries got married. Such a blending of cultures can be beautiful, but this ceremony included Christian traditions mixed with rituals from a faith that worshiped many gods.

Zephaniah the prophet pointedly condemned the mixing of other religions with faith in the one true God (sometimes called *syncretism*). Judah had become a people who bowed in worship to the true God but who also relied on the god Molek (Zephaniah 1:5). Zephaniah described their adoption of pagan culture (v. 8) and warned that as a result God would drive the people of Judah from their homeland.

Yet God never stopped loving His people. His judgment was meant to show them their need to turn to Him. So Zephaniah encouraged Judah to "Seek righteousness, seek humility" (2:3). Then the Lord gave them tender words promising future restoration: "At that time I will gather you; at that time I will bring you home" (3:20).

It's easy to condemn examples of obvious syncretism like the wedding I attended. But in reality, all of us easily blend God's truth with the assumptions of our culture. We need the Holy Spirit's guidance to test our beliefs against the truth of God's Word and then to stand for that truth confidently and lovingly. Our Father warmly embraces anyone who worships Him in the Spirit and in truth (see John 4:23–24).

MAKING IT WORK

Have you seen any examples of Christians engaging in activities that are not based in Scripture and incorporating them in the faith? Even if not, we need to be careful that how we live, how we worship, and how we raise our families is in line with Scripture and not some manmade version of it.

_____

_____

_____

_____

_____

_____

_____

_____

_____

_____

_____

_____

_____

_____

_____

Belonging

ISAIAH 44:1–5

~~~~~~~~

The LORD who made you and helps you says:
"Do not be afraid . . . my chosen one."

—**ISAIAH 44:2** NLT

I'd been out late the night before, just as I was every Saturday night. Just twenty years old, I was running from God as fast as I could. But suddenly, strangely, I felt compelled to attend the church my dad pastored. I put on my faded jeans, well-worn T-shirt, and unlaced high-tops and drove across town.

I don't recall the sermon Dad preached that day, but I'll never forget how delighted he was to see me. With his arm over my shoulder, he introduced me to everyone he saw. "This is my son!" he proudly declared. His joy became a picture of God's love that has stuck with me all these decades.

The imagery of God as loving Father occurs throughout the Bible. In Isaiah 44, the prophet interrupts a series of warnings to proclaim God's message of family love. "Dear Israel, my chosen one," he said. "I will pour out my Spirit on your descendants, and my blessing on your children" (vv. 2–3 NLT). Isaiah noted how the response of those descendants would demonstrate family pride. "Some will proudly claim, 'I belong to the

LORD,'" he wrote. "Some will write the LORD's name on their hands" (v. 5 NLT).

Wayward Israel belonged to God, just as I belonged to my father. Nothing I could do would ever make him lose his love for me. He gave me a glimpse of our heavenly Father's love for us.

MAKING IT WORK

Unconditional love is difficult, but it is the best way to show someone you care. Do you have a parent, sibling, spouse, or child who has drifted into a life that embraces ugodliness? The challenge is to love that person unconditionally with the idea of guiding them back to God. What can you do to show that kind of love?

_____

_____

_____

_____

_____

_____

_____

_____

_____

_____

_____

_____

_____

_____

_____

_____

_____

_____

God of the Depths

JOB 41:12–34

There is the sea, vast and spacious, . . .
and Leviathan, which you formed to frolic there.

—PSALM 104:25–26

"When you go to the deep sea, every time you take a sample, you'll find a new species," says marine biologist Ward Appeltans. In one recent year, scientists identified 1,451 new types of undersea life. We simply don't know the half of what's down there.

In Job 38–40, God reviewed His creation for Job's benefit. In three poetic chapters, God highlighted the wonders of weather, the vastness of the cosmos, and the variety of creatures in their habitats. These are things we can observe. Then God spoke of the mysterious Leviathan—for an entire chapter. Leviathan is a creature like no other, with harpoon-deflecting armor (Job 41:7, 13), graceful power (v. 12), and "fearsome teeth" (v. 14). "Flames stream from its mouth . . . smoke pours from its nostrils" (vv. 19–20). "Nothing on earth is its equal" (v. 33).

Okay, so God talks about a huge creature we haven't seen. Is that the point of Job 41?

No! Job 41 broadens our understanding of God's surprising character. The psalmist expanded on this when he wrote, "There is the sea, vast and spacious, . . . and Leviathan, which you formed to frolic there" (Psalm 104:25–26). After the terrifying description in Job, we learn that God created a playpen for this most fearsome of all creatures. Leviathan *frolics*.

We have the present to explore the ocean. We'll have eternity to explore the wonders of our magnificent, mysterious, playful God.

MAKING IT WORK

It takes some imagination to conjure up mind pictures of frolicking Leviathan. Likewise, trying to grasp the immensity of the universe God created or the intricate details of each human body can be daunting. The more you explore creation, the more you will grow in your awe of the One who created it.

_____

_____

_____

_____

_____

_____

_____

_____

_____

_____

_____

_____

_____

_____

_____

_____

Sight Unseen

LUKE 16:19–31

~~~~~~~~~

*If they do not listen to Moses and the Prophets, they will
not be convinced even if someone rises from the dead.*

—LUKE 16:31

After Yuri Gagarin became the first man in space in 1961, he
parachuted into the Russian countryside. A farmwoman spotted
the orange-clad cosmonaut, still wearing his helmet and dragging
two parachutes. "Can it be that you have come from outer space?"
she asked in surprise. "As a matter of fact, I have," he said.

Soviet leaders sadly turned the historic flight into antireligious
propaganda. "Gagarin went into space, but he didn't see any god
there," their premier declared. (Gagarin himself never said such a
thing.) As C. S. Lewis observed, "Those who do not find [God] on
earth are unlikely to find Him in space."

Jesus warned us about ignoring God in this life. He told a story
of two men who died—a rich man who had no time for God,
and Lazarus, a destitute man rich in faith (Luke 16:19–31). In
torment, the rich man pleaded with Abraham for his brothers still
on earth. "Send Lazarus," he begged Abraham. "If someone from
the dead goes to them, they will repent" (vv. 27, 30). Abraham got
to the heart of the problem: "If they do not listen to Moses and the

Prophets, they will not be convinced even if someone rises from the dead" (v. 31).

"Seeing is never believing," wrote Oswald Chambers. "We interpret what we see in the light of what we believe."

MAKING IT WORK

Our world wants to ignore God. How does that affect your life as you interact with people? Have you found it possible to talk about faith and God in ways that makes unbelievers at least listen and seek to learn? That is one of our biggest challenges.

_____

_____

_____

_____

_____

_____

_____

_____

_____

_____

_____

_____

_____

_____

_____

_____

_____

_____

On the Wrong Side?

PHILIPPIANS 1:12–18

～～～～

*What has happened to me has actually
served to advance the gospel.*

—PHILIPPIANS 1:12

When the bridge to Techiman, Ghana, washed out, residents of New Krobo on the other side of the Tano River were stranded. Attendance at Pastor Samuel Appiah's church in Techiman suffered too because many of the members lived in New Krobo—on the "wrong" side of the river.

Amid the crisis, Pastor Sam was trying to expand the church's children's home to care for more orphans. So he prayed. Then his church sponsored outdoor meetings across the river in New Krobo. Soon they were baptizing new believers in Jesus. A new church took root. Not only that, New Krobo had space to care for the orphans awaiting housing. God was weaving His restorative work into the crisis.

When the apostle Paul found himself on the "wrong" side of freedom, he didn't lament his situation. In a powerful letter to the church in Philippi, he wrote, "I want you to know, brothers and sisters, that what has happened to me has actually served to advance the gospel" (Philippians 1:12). Paul noted how his chains had led to "the whole palace guard" learning about Christ (v. 13). And others had gained confidence to share the good news of Jesus (v. 14).

Despite obstacles, Pastor Sam and the apostle Paul found God showing them new ways to work in their crises. What might God be doing in our challenging circumstances today?

MAKING IT WORK

As you review your life, what is the biggest challenge you face? Is it work related, family related, or faith related? Or something else? Do you have a trusted friend or acquaintance you could talk to about this? How can this challenge eventually be used to "advance the gospel"?

_____

_____

_____

_____

_____

_____

_____

_____

_____

_____

_____

_____

_____

_____

_____

_____

_____

_____

_____

Can't Die But Once

MATTHEW 10:26–32

*Do not be afraid of those who kill the body
but cannot kill the soul.*

— MATTHEW 10:28

Born into slavery and badly treated as a young girl, Harriet Tubman (c. 1822–1913) found a shining ray of hope in the Bible stories her mother told. The account of Israel's escape from slavery under Pharaoh showed her a God who desired freedom for His people.

Harriet found freedom when she slipped over the Maryland state line and out of slavery. She couldn't remain content, however, knowing so many were still trapped in captivity. So she led more than a dozen rescue missions to free those still in slavery, dismissing the personal danger. "I can't die but once," she said.

Harriet knew the truth of the statement: "Do not be afraid of those who kill the body but cannot kill the soul" (Matthew 10:28). Jesus spoke those words as He sent His disciples on their first mission. He knew they would face danger, and not everyone would receive them warmly. So why expose the disciples to the risk? The answer is found in the previous chapter. "When he saw the crowds, [Jesus] had compassion on them, because they were harassed and helpless, like sheep without a shepherd" (9:36).

When Harriet Tubman couldn't forget those still trapped in slavery, she showed us a picture of Christ, who did not forget us when we were trapped in our sins. Her courageous example inspires us to remember those who remain without hope in the world.

MAKING IT WORK

The heroism of a person like Harriet Tubman can't help but spur us on. She risked her life for others. Think of others in your life who need you to walk with them through something tough. Pick a couple of them and start a strategy of helping them.

_____

_____

_____

_____

_____

_____

_____

_____

_____

_____

_____

_____

_____

_____

_____

_____

It's Not About the Fish

JONAH 3:10–4:4

*When God saw what they did and how they
turned from their evil ways, he relented.*

—JONAH 3:10

Sighted numerous times off the coast of Australia's South
Queensland, Migaloo is the first albino humpback whale ever
documented. The splendid creature, estimated at more than
forty feet long, is so rare that Australia passed a law specifically
to protect him.

The Bible tells us about a "huge fish" so rare that God had
provided it especially to swallow a runaway prophet (Jonah
1:17). Most know the story. God told Jonah to take a message
of judgment to Nineveh. But Jonah wanted nothing to do with
the Ninevites, who had a reputation for cruelty to just about
everyone—including the Hebrews. So he fled. Things went badly.
From inside the fish, Jonah repented. Eventually he preached to
the Ninevites, and they repented too (3:5–10).

Great story, right? Except it doesn't end there. While Nineveh
repented, Jonah pouted. "Isn't this what I said, LORD?" he prayed.
"I knew that you are a gracious and compassionate God, slow
to anger and abounding in love" (4:2). Despite being rescued

from certain death, Jonah let his sinful anger grew until even his prayer became suicidal (see v. 3).

The story of Jonah isn't about the fish. It's about our human nature and the nature of the God who pursues us. "The Lord . . . is patient with you," wrote the apostle Peter, "not wanting anyone to perish, but everyone to come to repentance" (2 Peter 3:9). God offers His love to brutal Ninevites, pouting prophets, and you and me.

MAKING IT WORK

How are we sometimes like Jonah? And what do we learn about God through His dealings with Jonah? We often think the star of the story is the big fish, but it's really about God and His desire for everyone to trust Him. Who do you know who needs to discover God's love?

_____

_____

_____

_____

_____

_____

_____

_____

_____

_____

_____

_____

_____

_____

_____

_____

God's Brand

ZECHARIAH 3:1–7

∽∽∽

I have taken away your sin,
and I will put fine garments on you.

— ZECHARIAH 3:4

Scooping up the smallest children, a frantic maid raced out of the flaming house. As she ran, she called loudly to five-year-old Jacky.

But Jacky didn't follow. Outside, a bystander reacted quickly. Standing on the shoulders of a friend and reaching into the upstairs window, he pulled Jacky to safety—just before the roof caved in. Little Jacky, said his mother Susanna, was "a brand [stick] plucked from the burning." You might know that "brand" as the great traveling minister John Wesley (1703–1791).

Susanna Wesley was quoting Zechariah, a prophet who provides valuable insight into God's character. Relating a vision he had, the prophet takes us into a courtroom scene where Satan is standing next to Joshua the high priest (3:1). Satan accuses Joshua, but the Lord rebukes the devil and says, "Is this not a brand [burning stick] plucked from the fire?" (v. 2 NKJV). The Lord tells Joshua, "I have taken away your sin, and I will put fine garments on you" (v. 4).

Then the Lord gave Joshua this challenge—and an opportunity: "If you will walk in obedience to me and keep my requirements, then you will govern my house" (v. 7).

What a picture of the gift we receive from God through our faith in Jesus! He snatches us from the fire, cleans us up, and works in us as we follow His Spirit's leading. You might call us God's brands plucked from the fire.

MAKING IT WORK

Think of how God has "snatched you from the fire," so to speak. Imagine what your life would be like without Jesus. How might your life have been different. Perhaps this will give you the impetus to spend some time in praise for what God has done in your life.

_____

_____

_____

_____

_____

_____

_____

_____

_____

_____

_____

_____

_____

_____

_____

_____

Where Is Peace?

JEREMIAH 8:8–15

~~~~~~~~

We have peace with God through our Lord Jesus Christ.

— ROMANS 5:1

"Do you still hope for peace?" a journalist asked singer-songwriter Bob Dylan in 1984. "There is not going to be any peace," Dylan replied. His response drew criticism, yet there's no denying that peace remains ever elusive.

About six hundred years before Christ, most prophets were predicting peace. God's prophet wasn't one of them. Jeremiah reminded the people that God had said, "Obey me, and I will be your God and you will be my people" (Jeremiah 7:23). Yet they repeatedly ignored the Lord and His commands. Their false prophets said, "Peace, peace" (8:11), but Jeremiah predicted disaster. Jerusalem fell in 586 BC.

Peace is rare. But amid Jeremiah's book of dire prophecies we discover a God who loves relentlessly. "I have loved you with an everlasting love," the Lord told His rebellious people. "I will build you up again" (31:3–4).

God is a God of love and peace. Conflict comes because of our rebellion against Him. Sin destroys the world's peace and robs each of us of inner peace. Jesus came to this planet to reconcile us to God and give us that inner peace. "Since we have been justified through faith, we have peace with God through our Lord Jesus Christ," wrote the apostle Paul (Romans 5:1). His words are among the most hope-filled ever written.

Whether we live in a combat zone or dwell in a serene neighborhood with nary a whisper of war, Christ invites us into His peace.

MAKING IT WORK

What is peaceful to you about your relationship with God? Is there any aspect of your life that is not peaceful but that you feel could change if you were to allow the Holy Spirit to work in you to fix that area? Why not ask Him to help you make that change?

_____

_____

_____

_____

_____

_____

_____

_____

_____

_____

_____

_____

_____

_____

_____

_____

Zax Nature

PHILIPPIANS 4:1–7

~~~~~~~~~~

Let your gentleness be evident to all.

— PHILIPPIANS 4:5

In one of Dr. Seuss's whimsical stories, he tells of a "North-Going Zax and a South-Going Zax" crossing the Prairie of Prax. Upon meeting nose to nose, neither Zax will step aside. The first Zax angrily vows to stay put—even if it makes "the whole world stand still." (Unfazed, the world moves on and builds a highway around them.)

The tale offers an uncomfortably accurate picture of human nature. We possess a reflexive "need" to be right, and we're prone to stubbornly cling to that instinct in rather destructive ways!

Happily for us, God lovingly chooses to soften stubborn human hearts. The apostle Paul knew this, so when two members of the Philippian church were squabbling, he loved them enough to call them out (Philippians 4:2). Then, having earlier instructed the believers to "have the same mindset" of self-giving love as Christ (2:5–8), Paul asked them to "help these women," valued coworkers with him in sharing the gospel (4:3). It seems that peacemaking and wise compromise call for team effort.

Of course there are times to take a firm stand, but a Christlike approach will look a lot different than an unyielding Zax! So many things in life aren't worth fighting over. We can bicker with each other over every trivial concern until we destroy ourselves (Galatians 5:15). Or we can swallow our pride, graciously receive wise counsel, and seek unity with our brothers and sisters.

MAKING IT WORK

What are some issues that you find Christians grumbling about and sometimes breaking fellowship over? How does social media help us to do this to the detriment of Christian unity? How can you be part of the solution for finding unity in the church?

_____

_____

_____

_____

_____

_____

_____

_____

_____

_____

_____

_____

_____

_____

_____

_____

_____

Trying to Impress

MATTHEW 15:1–11, 16–20

Out of the heart come evil thoughts. . . .
These are what defile a person.

— MATTHEW 15:19–20

When a college class went on a cultural field trip, the instructor almost didn't recognize one of his star pupils. In the classroom she had concealed six-inch heels beneath her pant legs. But in her walking boots she was less than five feet tall. "My heels are how I want to be," she laughed. "But my boots are how I really am."

Our physical appearance doesn't define who we are; it's our heart that matters. Jesus had strong words for those masters of appearances—the super-religious "Pharisees and teachers of the law." They asked Jesus why His disciples didn't wash their hands before eating, as their religious traditions dictated (Matthew 15:1–2). Jesus asked, "Why do you break the command of God for the sake of your tradition?" (v. 3). Then He pointed out how they had invented a legal loophole to keep their wealth instead of caring for their parents (vv. 4–6), thus dishonoring them and violating the fifth commandment (Exodus 20:12).

If we obsess over appearances while looking for loopholes in God's clear commands, we're violating the spirit of His law.

Jesus said that "out of the heart come evil thoughts—murder, adultery, sexual immorality," and the like (Matthew 15:19). Only God, through the righteousness of His Son Jesus, can give us a clean heart.

MAKING IT WORK

Are you looking for (and maybe finding) loopholes that you think allow you to skip some of God's life guides that are clearly pointed out in Scripture? Consider how those loopholes might be damaging important relationships in your life. Why not pick one of them and begin working to close that loophole in the coming days?

_____

_____

_____

_____

_____

_____

_____

_____

_____

_____

_____

_____

_____

_____

_____

_____

_____

_____

_____

_____

The Battle

PSALM 39:1–7

~~~~~~~~~

But now, Lord, what do I look for? My hope is in you.

— PSALM 39:7

As artillery rounds crashed around him with an earth-shaking *whoomp*, the young soldier prayed fervently, "Lord, if you get me through this, I'll go to that Bible school Mom wanted me to attend." God honored his focused prayer. My dad survived World War II, went to Moody Bible Institute, and invested his life in ministry.

Another warrior endured a different kind of crisis that drove him to God, but his problems arose when he avoided combat. As King David's troops fought the Ammonites, David was back at his palace casting more than just a glance at another man's wife (see 2 Samuel 11). In Psalm 39, David chronicles the painful process of restoration from the terrible sin that resulted. "The turmoil within me grew worse," he wrote. "The more I thought about it, the hotter I got" (vv. 2–3 NLT).

David's broken spirit caused him to reflect: "Show me, LORD, my life's end and the number of my days; let me know how fleeting my life is" (v. 4). Amid his renewed focus, David didn't despair. He had nowhere else to turn. "But now, Lord, what do I look for? My hope is in you" (v. 7). David would survive this personal battle and go on to serve God.

What motivates our prayer life doesn't matter as much as the focus of our prayer. God is our source of hope. He wants us to share our heart with Him.

MAKING IT WORK

What an amazing admission by David in Psalm 39:2–3: "The more I thought about [my turmoil], the hotter I got" (NLT). Have you ever been there? That's what dealing with sin can do inside us—causing an intense friction in our heart, so to speak. Anything going on like that in your heart? Give it to God and cool off.

_____

_____

_____

_____

_____

_____

_____

_____

_____

_____

_____

_____

_____

_____

_____

_____

_____

_____

More Than a Symbol

2 SAMUEL 23:13–17

~~~~~~~~~~

*In humility value others above yourselves, not looking to your
own interests but each of you to the interests of the others.*

— PHILIPPIANS 2:3–4

On the verge of making team history, University of Iowa basketball star Jordan Bohannon intentionally missed the free throw that would have broken a twenty-five-year-old school record. Why? In 1993, days after Iowa's Chris Street had made his thirty-fourth free throw in a row, he lost his life in a car crash. Bohannon chose to honor Street's memory by not breaking his record.

Bohannon showed a keen awareness of things more important than his own advancement. We see similar values in the life of the young warrior David. Hiding in a cave with his ragtag army, David longed for a drink from the well in his hometown of Bethlehem, but the dreaded Philistines occupied the area (2 Samuel 23:14–15).

In a stunning act of bravery, three of David's warriors "broke through the Philistine lines," got the water, and brought it to David. But David couldn't bring himself to drink it. Instead, he "poured it out before the LORD," saying, "Is it not the blood of men who went at the risk of their lives?" (vv. 16–17).

In a world that often rewards those who seize whatever they can grasp, our acts of love and sacrifice can be so powerful! Such deeds are much more than mere symbols.

MAKING IT WORK

Leadership calls for discernment, wisdom, and surprisingly, humility and sacrifice. Who are some examples of people you know who have those traits? In what forms of leadership in your life can you demonstrate such godly leadership skills?

_____

_____

_____

_____

_____

_____

_____

_____

_____

_____

_____

_____

_____

_____

_____

_____

_____

_____

_____

In the Moment

LUKE 23:32–46

~~~~~~~~~

The reason my Father loves me is that I lay down my life. . . .
No one takes it from me, but I lay it down of my own accord.

—JOHN 10:17–18

The ambulance door was about to close—with me on the inside. Outside, my son was on the phone to my wife. From my concussed fog, I called his name. As he recalls the moment, I slowly said, "Tell your mom I love her very much."

Apparently I thought this might be goodbye, and I wanted those to be my parting words. In the moment, that's what mattered most to me.

As Jesus endured His darkest moment, He didn't merely tell us He loved us; He showed it in specific ways. He showed it to the mocking soldiers who had just nailed Him to a cross: "Father, forgive them, for they do not know what they are doing" (Luke 23:34). He gave hope to a criminal crucified with Him: "Today you will be with me in paradise" (v. 43). Nearing the end, He looked at His mother. "Here is your son," He said to her, and to His close friend John He said, "Here is your mother" (John 19:26–27). Then, as His life slipped from Him, Jesus's last act of love was to trust His Father: "Into your hands I commit my spirit" (Luke 23:46).

Jesus purposefully chose the cross in order to show His obedience to His Father—and the depth of His love for us. To the very end, He showed us His relentless love.

MAKING IT WORK

Jesus's love for us was relentless as He burst through all of the darkness of His impending death to bring life to us. On a smaller scale (infinitely smaller), we show love for others by breaking through obstacles. What stands in your way of showing relentless love to your wife or your children? What can you do about it?

_____

_____

_____

_____

_____

_____

_____

_____

_____

_____

_____

_____

_____

_____

_____

_____

_____

_____

_____

"Jesus purposefully
chose the cross
in order to show
His obedience to His Father—
and the depth
of His love for us."

The Heart of Fasting

ZECHARIAH 7:1–10

~~~~~~

*The fasts . . . will become joyful and glad occasions
and happy festivals for Judah. Therefore love truth and peace.*

—ZECHARIAH 8:19

Hunger pangs gnawed at my nerves. My mentor had recommended fasting as a way to focus on God. But as the day wore on, I wondered: How did Jesus do this for forty days? I struggled to rely on the Holy Spirit for peace, strength, and patience. Especially patience.

If we're physically able, fasting can teach us the importance of our spiritual food. As Jesus said, "Man shall not live on bread alone, but on every word that comes from the mouth of God" (Matthew 4:4). Yet, as I learned firsthand, fasting on its own doesn't necessarily draw us closer to God!

In fact, God once told His people through the prophet Zechariah that their practice of fasting was useless since it wasn't leading to service for the poor. "Was it really for me that you fasted?" God asked pointedly (Zechariah 7:5).

God's question revealed that the primary problem wasn't their stomachs; it was their cold hearts. By continuing to serve themselves, they were failing to draw closer to God's heart. So He urged them, "Administer true justice; show mercy and compassion to one another. Do not oppress the widow or the fatherless, the foreigner or the poor" (vv. 9–10).

Our goal in any spiritual discipline is to draw closer to Jesus. As we grow in likeness to Him, we'll gain a heart for those He loves.

MAKING IT WORK

What is the hardest spiritual discipline for you? Some of the things we can be doing: studying God's Word, praying, worshiping, enjoying the company of good friends. What plan can you establish to use the disciplines of the spiritual life to grow closer to the Lord?

_____

_____

_____

_____

_____

_____

_____

_____

_____

_____

_____

_____

_____

_____

_____

_____

_____

_____

Rescuing Villains

DANIEL 3:26–30

Praise be to the God of Shadrach, Meshach and Abednego,
who has sent his angel and rescued his servants!

— DANIEL 3:28

The comic book hero is as popular as ever. In one recent year, six superhero movies accounted for more than $4 billion in box office sales. But why are people so drawn to big action flicks?

Maybe it's because, in part, such stories resemble God's Big Story. There's a hero, a villain, a people in need of rescue, and plenty of riveting action.

In God's story, the biggest villain is Satan, the enemy of our souls. But there are lots of "little" villains as well. In the book of Daniel, for example, one is Nebuchadnezzar, the king of much of the known world, who decided to kill anyone who didn't worship his giant statue (Daniel 3:1–6). When three courageous Jewish officials refused (vv. 12–18), God dramatically rescued them from a blazing furnace (vv. 24–27).

But in a surprising twist, we see this villain's heart begin to change. In response to this spectacular event, Nebuchadnezzar said, "Praise be to the God of Shadrach, Meshach and Abednego" (v. 28).

Then he threatened to kill anyone who defied God (v. 29), not yet understanding that God didn't need his help. Nebuchadnezzar would learn more about God in chapter 4—but that's another story.

What we see in Nebuchadnezzar isn't just a villain, but someone on a spiritual journey. In God's story of redemption, our hero, Jesus, reaches out to everyone needing rescue—including villains like you and me.

MAKING IT WORK

If you want to read about a "villain" who was miraculously saved by Jesus and who became a great statesman for Christianity and the United States, get a copy of the book *Born Again* by Charles Colson. Colson did a lot of dirty work for President Richard Nixon—and then his life was transformed by Jesus.

Whatever the Cost

JOHN 12:37–43

～～～～

They would not openly acknowledge their faith for fear.

—JOHN 12:42

The film *Paul, Apostle of Christ* takes an unflinching look at persecution in the early days of the church. Even the movie's minor characters reveal how dangerous it was to follow Jesus. Consider these roles listed in the credits: Beaten Woman; Beaten Man; Christian Victims 1, 2, and 3.

Identifying with Christ often came at a high cost. And in much of the world, it's still dangerous to follow Jesus. Many in the church today can relate to that kind of persecution. Some of us, however, may feel "persecuted" prematurely—outraged any time our faith is mocked or we suspect we were passed over for a promotion because of our beliefs.

Obviously, there's a colossal difference between sacrificing social status and sacrificing our lives. Realistically, though, self-interest, financial stability, and social acceptance have always been intense human motivators. We see this in the actions of some of Jesus's earliest converts. The apostle John reports that mere days before Jesus's crucifixion, although most Israelites were still rejecting Him (John 12:37), many "even among the leaders believed"

(v. 42). However, "They would not openly acknowledge their faith . . . for they loved human praise more than praise from God" (vv. 42–43).

Today we still face societal pressures (and worse) to keep our faith in Christ hidden. Whatever the cost, let's stand together as a people who seek God's approval more than human praise.

MAKING IT WORK

What are some of the pressures you face relating to your faith? What are some negative results of letting people in your sphere of influence know that you are a Christian? Could you talk with some other Christian guys about how to witness effectively in those situations?

_____

_____

_____

_____

_____

_____

_____

_____

_____

_____

_____

_____

_____

_____

_____

_____

_____

Who Am I?

EXODUS 3:10–17

~~~~~~

"I AM WHO I AM."

— EXODUS 3:14

Dave enjoyed his job, but for a long time he had sensed a pull toward something else. Now he was about to fulfill his dream and step into missions work. But strangely, he began to have serious doubts.

"I don't deserve this," he told a friend. "The mission board doesn't know the real me. I'm not good enough."

Dave has some pretty good company. Mention the name of Moses and we think of leadership, strength, and the Ten Commandments. We might forget that Moses fled to the desert after murdering a man. We lose sight of his forty years as a fugitive. We overlook his anger problem and his intense reluctance to say yes to God.

When God showed up with marching orders (Exodus 3:1–10), Moses played the I'm-not-good-enough card. He even got into a lengthy argument with God, asking Him: "Who am I?" (v. 11). Then God told Moses who He was: "I AM WHO I AM" (v. 14). It's impossible for us to adequately explain that mysterious name, because with that name our indescribable God is describing to Moses His eternal existence.

A sense of our own weaknesses is healthy. But if we use them as excuses to keep God from using us, we insult Him. What we're really saying is that God isn't good enough.

The question isn't Who am I? The question is Who is the I AM?

MAKING IT WORK

How often do you feel like Moses (*I am not the man for this task, Lord*)? What do we find out about God in this incident that helps us depend on Him rather than on ourselves when facing a major task for God's kingdom?

_____

_____

_____

_____

_____

_____

_____

_____

_____

_____

_____

_____

_____

_____

_____

_____

_____

_____

_____

Just a Touch

REVELATION 1:9–18

~~~~~~~~

Then he placed his right hand on me and said,
"Do not be afraid. I am the First and the Last."

— REVELATION 1:17

It was just a touch, but it made all the difference to Colin. As his small team was preparing to do charitable work in a region known for hostility to believers in Jesus, his stress level began to rise. When he shared his worries with a teammate, his friend stopped, placed his hand on his shoulder, and shared a few encouraging words with him. Colin now looks back on that brief touch as a turning point, a powerful reminder of the simple truth that God was with him.

John, the close friend and disciple of Jesus, had been banished to the desolate island of Patmos for preaching the gospel, when he heard "a loud voice like a trumpet" (Revelation 1:10). That startling event was followed by a vision of the Lord himself, and John "fell at his feet as though dead." But in that frightening moment, he received comfort and courage. John wrote, "He placed his right hand on me and said: 'Do not be afraid. I am the First and the Last'" (v. 17).

God takes us out of our comfort zone to show us new things, to stretch us, to help us grow. But He also brings the courage and comfort to go through every situation. He won't leave us alone in our trials. He has everything under control. His hand is on our shoulder.

MAKING IT WORK

What a great place to be—our comfort zone. And sometimes we need a place to rest and replenish. But sometimes the door opens, and God wants us to step out of our safe place. What do you think God is calling you to do that is difficult? How can you begin to prepare to face this challenge?

_____

_____

_____

_____

_____

_____

_____

_____

_____

_____

_____

_____

_____

_____

_____

_____

_____

_____

_____

Lava in Paradise

2 SAMUEL 6:1–9

~~~~~~

*Let us then approach God's throne of grace
with confidence, so that we may receive mercy
and find grace to help us in our time of need.*

— HEBREWS 4:16

All is quiet, save for slowly stretching tentacles of hissing lava nipping at the edges of the tropical foliage. Residents stand grim-faced yet amazed. Most days they call this "paradise." On this day, however, the fiery fissures in Hawaii's Puna district reminded everyone that God forged these islands via untamable volcanic power.

The ancient Israelites encountered an untamable power too. When King David recaptured the ark of the covenant (2 Samuel 6:1–4), a celebration broke out (v. 5)—until a man died suddenly when he grabbed hold of the ark to steady it (vv. 6–7).

This may tempt us to think of God as being as unpredictable as a volcano, just as likely to create as He is to destroy. However, it will help us to remember that God had given Israel specific instructions for how to handle the things set apart for worshiping Him (see Numbers 4). Israel had the privilege of drawing near to God, but His presence was too overwhelming for them to approach Him carelessly.

Hebrews 12 recalls a mountain "burning with fire" (v. 19), where God gave Moses the Ten Commandments. That mountain terrified everyone (vv. 18–21). But the writer contrasts that scene with this: "You have come to . . . Jesus the mediator of a new covenant" (vv. 22–24). Jesus—God's very Son—made the way for us to draw near to His untamable yet loving Father.

MAKING IT WORK

What stands out to you about God as you read the third paragraph above? Why is God presented as overwhelming to approach in the Old Testament and so accessible in the New Testament? Does His accessibility encourage you to pray? What steps can you take to pray more?

_____

_____

_____

_____

_____

_____

_____

_____

_____

_____

_____

_____

_____

_____

_____

_____

The Flip Side of Love

2 JOHN 1:1–11

~~~~~~

Grace, mercy and peace from God the Father and from Jesus Christ, the Father's Son, will be with us in truth and love.

— 2 JOHN 1:3

Roman inns during the time of Christ had a reputation so bad that rabbis wouldn't even permit cattle to be left at them. Faced with such bad conditions, traveling Christians usually sought out other believers for hospitality.

Among those early travelers were false teachers who denied that Jesus was the Messiah. This is why the letter of 2 John tells its readers there is a time to refuse to extend hospitality. John had said in a previous letter that these false teachers were "antichrist—denying the Father and the Son" (1 John 2:22). In 2 John 1 he elaborated on this, telling his readers that whoever believes Jesus is the Messiah "has both the Father and the Son" (v. 9).

Then he warned, "If anyone comes to you and does not bring this teaching, do not take them into your house or welcome them" (v. 10). To extend hospitality to someone preaching a false gospel would actually help keep people separated from God.

John's second letter shows us a "flip side" of God's love. We serve a God who welcomes everyone with open arms. But genuine love won't enable those who deceitfully harm themselves and others. God wraps His arms around those who come to Him in repentance, but He never embraces a lie.

MAKING IT WORK

Have you ever encountered a false teacher—someone who is teaching ideas that are heretical in regard to true biblical teaching? How equipped are you to recognize teaching that is unbiblical? Is there anything you could do to be more equipped?

_____

_____

_____

_____

_____

_____

_____

_____

_____

_____

_____

_____

_____

_____

_____

_____

_____

_____

_____

_____

Abba, Father

ROMANS 8:12–17

~~~~~~

A father to the fatherless, a defender
of widows, is God in his holy dwelling.

— PSALM 68:5

The scene belonged on one of those hilarious Father's Day cards. As a dad muscled a lawn mower ahead of him with one hand, he expertly towed a child's wagon behind him with the other. In the wagon sat his three-year-old daughter, delighted at the noisy tour of their yard. Who says men can't multitask?

If you had a good dad, a scene like that can invoke fantastic memories. But for many, "Dad" is an incomplete concept. Where are we to turn if our fathers are gone, or if they fail us, or even if they wound us?

King David certainly had his shortcomings as a father, but he understood the paternal nature of God. "A father to the fatherless," he wrote, "a defender of widows, is God in his holy dwelling. God sets the lonely in families" (Psalm 68:5–6). The apostle Paul expanded on that idea: "The Spirit you received brought about your adoption to sonship." Then, using the Aramaic word for father—a term young children would use for their dad—Paul added, "By him we cry, 'Abba, Father'" (Romans 8:15). This is the same word

Jesus used when He prayed in anguish to His Father the night He was betrayed (Mark 14:36).

What a privilege to come to God using the same intimate term for "father" that Jesus used! Our Abba Father welcomes into His family anyone who will turn to Him.

MAKING IT WORK

If you think of our Almighty God in terms somewhat similar to how you think of an earthly father, what changes for you? What provisions, help, and comfort does a good earthside father have that sound like what you want from God as Father?

_____

_____

_____

_____

_____

_____

_____

_____

_____

_____

_____

_____

_____

_____

_____

_____

_____

_____

_____

_____

The Forecaster's Mistake

JEREMIAH 23:16–22

~~~~~~~

Let the one who has my word speak it faithfully.

— JEREMIAH 23:28

At noon on September 21, 1938, a young meteorologist warned the US Weather Bureau of two fronts forcing a hurricane northward toward New England. But the chief of forecasting scoffed at Charles Pierce's prediction. Surely a tropical storm wouldn't strike so far north.

Two hours later, the 1938 New England Hurricane made landfall on Long Island. By 4:00 p.m. it had reached New England, tossing ships onto land as homes crumbled into the sea. More than six hundred people died. Had the victims received Pierce's warning—based on solid data and his detailed maps—they likely would have survived.

The concept of knowing whose word to heed has precedent in Scripture. In Jeremiah's day, God warned His people against false prophets. "Do not listen [to them]," He said. "They fill you with false hopes. They speak visions from their own minds, not from the mouth of the LORD" (Jeremiah 23:16). God said of them, "If they had stood in my council, they would have proclaimed my words to my people" (v. 22).

"False prophets" are still with us. "Experts" dispense advice while ignoring God altogether or twisting His words to suit their purposes. But through His Word and Spirit, God has given us what we need to begin to discern the false from the true. As we gauge everything by the truth of His Word, our own words and lives will increasingly reflect that truth to others.

MAKING IT WORK

What is the best way to speak about God's truth to others? Do they see it best in our lives—what we say, how we treat others, our faithfulness? Or do they respond best to our words of witness? Which works best for you when you want to let someone know about God?

_____

_____

_____

_____

_____

_____

_____

_____

_____

_____

_____

_____

_____

_____

_____

_____

_____

Shocking Honesty

1 PETER 3:7–12

~~~~~~

*Treat [your wife] as you should
so your prayers will not be hindered.*

—1 PETER 3:7 NLT

When the minister asked one of his elders to lead the congregation in prayer, the man shocked everyone. "I'm sorry, Pastor," he said, "but I've been arguing with my wife all the way to church, and I'm in no condition to pray." The next moment was awkward. The minister prayed. The service moved on. Later, the pastor vowed never to ask anyone to pray publicly without first asking privately.

That man demonstrated astonishing honesty in a place where hypocrisy would have been easier. But there is a larger lesson about prayer here. God is a loving Father. If I as a husband do not respect and honor my wife—a cherished daughter of God—why would her heavenly Father hear my prayers?

The apostle Peter made an interesting observation about this. He instructed husbands to treat their wives with respect and as equal heirs in Christ "so that nothing will hinder your prayers" (1 Peter 3:7). The underlying principle is that our relationships affect our prayer life.

What would happen if we exchanged the Sunday smiles and the façade of religiosity for refreshing honesty with our brothers and sisters? What might God do through us when we pray and learn to love each other as we love ourselves?

MAKING IT WORK

Married? Then think a minute about the line above that calls your wife "a cherished daughter of God." Do you love her as much as you love yourself? Can she see that by what you say and do? Could you have prayed if the pastor had asked you to pray?

_____

_____

_____

_____

_____

_____

_____

_____

_____

_____

_____

_____

_____

_____

_____

_____

_____

_____

_____

"God Stuff"

1 PETER 3:13–18

Always be prepared to give an answer to everyone who asks you to give the reason for the hope that you have.

— 1 PETER 3:15

Most of Mike's coworkers knew little about Christianity, nor did they seem to care. But they knew he cared. One day near the Easter season, someone casually mentioned that they'd heard Easter had something to do with Passover and wondered what the connection was. "Hey, Mike!" he said. "You know about this God stuff. What's Passover?"

So Mike explained how God brought the Israelites out of slavery in Egypt. He told them about the ten plagues, including the death of the firstborn in every household. He explained how the death angel "passed over" the houses whose doorframes were covered by the blood of a sacrificed lamb. Then he shared how Jesus was later crucified at the Passover season as the once-and-for-all sacrificial Lamb. Suddenly Mike realized, *Hey, I'm witnessing!*

Peter the disciple gave advice to a church in a culture that didn't know about God. He said, "Always be prepared to give an answer to everyone who asks you to give the reason for the hope that you have" (1 Peter 3:15).

Because Mike had been open about his faith, he got the chance to share that faith naturally, and he could do so with "gentleness and respect" (v. 15).

We can too. With the help of God's Holy Spirit, we can explain in simple terms what matters most in life—that "stuff" about God.

MAKING IT WORK

How comfortable are you talking about "God stuff" with others? Do you know anyone who is pretty good at it? Could you talk to him and see what works for him? Ask him for some pointers, perhaps?

_____

_____

_____

_____

_____

_____

_____

_____

_____

_____

_____

_____

_____

_____

_____

_____

_____

_____

_____

Pride at the Core

EZRA 9:1–9

～～～

Ezra . . . was a teacher well versed in the Law of Moses.

—EZRA 7:6

"He thinks he's really something!" That was my friend's assessment of a fellow Christian we knew. We thought we saw in him a spirit of pride. We were saddened when we learned that he soon was caught in some serious misdeeds. By elevating himself, he had found nothing but trouble. We realized that could happen to us as well.

It can be easy to minimize the terrible sin of pride in our own hearts. The more we learn and the more success we enjoy, the more likely we are to think we're "really something." Pride is at the core of our nature.

In Scripture, Ezra is described as "a teacher well versed in the Law of Moses" (Ezra 7:6). King Artaxerxes appointed him to lead an expedition of Hebrew exiles back to Jerusalem. Ezra could have been a prime candidate to succumb to the sin of pride. Yet he didn't. Ezra not only knew God's law but he also lived it.

After his arrival in Jerusalem, Ezra learned that Jewish men had married women who served other gods, defying God's express directions (9:1–2). He tore his clothes in grief and prayed in heartfelt repentance (vv. 5–15). A higher purpose guided Ezra's knowledge and position: his love for God and for His people. He prayed, "Here we are before you in our guilt, though because of it not one of us can stand in your presence" (v. 15).

Ezra understood the scope of their sins. But in humility he repented and trusted in the goodness of our forgiving God.

MAKING IT WORK

What do you think about pride? Is pride always a sin? Isn't it okay to have pride in a job well done? Or to have pride in your family and the great things your kids do? How do we have pride without being arrogant or selfish?

_____

_____

_____

_____

_____

_____

_____

_____

_____

_____

_____

_____

_____

_____

_____

_____

_____

Fire in the Desert

EXODUS 3:1–10

～～～～

I am sending you to Pharaoh to bring
my people the Israelites out of Egypt.

— EXODUS 3:10

While riding in the Chihuahuan Desert in the late 1800s, Jim White spotted a strange cloud of smoke spiraling skyward. Suspecting a wildfire, the young cowboy rode toward the source, only to learn that the "smoke" was a vast swarm of bats spilling from a hole in the ground. White had come across New Mexico's Carlsbad Caverns, an immense and spectacular system of caves.

As Moses was tending sheep in a Middle Eastern desert, he too saw an odd sight that grabbed his attention—a flaming bush that didn't burn up (Exodus 3:2). When God himself spoke from the bush, Moses realized he had come to something far grander than it had first appeared. The Lord told Moses, "I am the God of your father, the God of Abraham" (v. 6). God was about to lead an enslaved people to freedom and show them their true identity as His children (v. 10).

More than six hundred years earlier, God had made this promise to Abraham: "All peoples on earth will be blessed through you" (Genesis 12:3). The flight of the Israelites from Egypt was but one step in that blessing—God's plan to rescue His creation through the Messiah, Abraham's descendant.

Today we can enjoy the benefits of that blessing, for God offers this rescue to everyone. Christ came to die for the sins of the whole world. By faith in Him, we too become children of the living God.

MAKING IT WORK

However you praise God, wouldn't it be a great time now to thank Him for salvation—the greatest blessing of this life? How can you encourage your family to praise God together for what He has done?

_____

_____

_____

_____

_____

_____

_____

_____

_____

_____

_____

_____

_____

_____

_____

_____

_____

What Do We Want?

ROMANS 8:1–11

~~~~~~~

He who raised Christ from the dead will also give life to your mortal bodies because of his Spirit who lives in you.

—**ROMANS 8:11**

"I went from the horse-and-buggy to a man walking on the moon," said the elderly man to his granddaughter, who shared this story with me recently. But then he mused, "I never thought it would be so short."

Life is short, and many of us turn to Jesus because we want to live forever. That's not bad, but we don't comprehend what eternal life really is. We tend to crave the wrong things. We long for something better, and we think it's just ahead. If only I were out of school. If only I had that job. If only I were married. If only I could retire. If only . . . And then one day we catch an echo of our grandfather's voice as we wonder where the time has flown.

The truth is, we possess eternal life now. The apostle Paul wrote, "The law of the Spirit who gives life has set you free from the law of sin and death" (Romans 8:2). Then he said, "Those who live in accordance with the Spirit have their minds set on what the Spirit desires" (v. 5). In other words, our desires change when we come to Christ. This naturally gives us what we most desire. "The mind governed by the Spirit is life and peace" (v. 6).

It's one of life's great lies that we need to be somewhere else, doing something else, with someone else before we start truly living. When we find our life in Jesus, we exchange regret over life's brevity for the full enjoyment of life with Him, both now and forever.

MAKING IT WORK

Do you ever feel that you are in the prison of unfulfilled expectations? The "if only" syndrome? A true trust in God can free you from that and allow you to use today's circumstances for God's glory and your own contentment. You've already begun your eternal life. Enjoy it.

~~~~~

"It's one of life's great lies
that we need to be
somewhere else,
doing something else,
with someone else
before we start truly living."

~~~~~

Space for Me

MARK 3:13–19

〜〜〜〜

*Jesus went up on a mountainside and called to him
those he wanted, and they came to him.*

—MARK 3:13

He was an aging military veteran, rough-edged and given to even
rougher language. One day a friend cared enough about him to
inquire about his spiritual beliefs. The man's dismissive response
came quickly: "God doesn't have space for someone like me."

Perhaps that was just part of his "tough-guy" act, but his words
couldn't be further from the truth! God creates space especially for
the rough, the guilt-ridden, and the excluded to belong and thrive
in His community. This was obvious from the beginning of Jesus's
ministry, when He made some surprising choices for His disciples. First, He chose several fishermen from Galilee—the "wrong
side of the tracks" from the perspective of those in Jerusalem. He
also selected a tax collector, Matthew, whose profession included
extorting from his oppressed countrymen. Then, for good measure, Jesus invited the "other" Simon—"the Zealot" (Mark 3:18).

We don't know much about this Simon (he isn't Simon Peter),
but we do know about the Zealots. They hated traitors like Matthew, who got rich by collaborating with the despised Romans.

Yet with divine irony, Jesus chose Simon along with Matthew, brought them together, and blended them into His team.

Don't write anyone off as too "bad" for Jesus. After all, He said, "I have not come to call the righteous, but sinners to repentance" (Luke 5:32). He has plenty of space for the tough cases—people like you and me.

MAKING IT WORK

You probably encounter some people who seem too far gone to be saved. Maybe there are people you don't know but are aware of from the news or other media. Would it be good to at least make those people items of prayer—because we know God can save them?

_____

_____

_____

_____

_____

_____

_____

_____

_____

_____

_____

_____

_____

_____

_____

_____

_____

_____

Ripple Effect

EZRA 8:15–21

Because the hand of the LORD my God was on me, I took
courage and gathered leaders from Israel to go up with me.

— EZRA 7:28

The little Bible college in northern Ghana didn't look impressive—just a tin-roofed cinder-block building and a handful of students. Yet Bob Hayes poured his life into those students. He gave them leadership roles and encouraged them to preach and teach, despite their occasional reluctance. Bob passed away years ago, but dozens of thriving churches, schools, and two additional Bible institutes have sprung up across Ghana—all started by graduates of that humble school.

During the reign of King Artaxerxes (465–424 BC), Ezra the scribe assembled a band of Jewish exiles to return to Jerusalem. But Ezra found no Levites among them (Ezra 8:15). He needed Levites to serve as priests. So he commissioned leaders to "bring attendants to us for the house of our God" (v. 17). They did so (vv. 18–20), and Ezra led them all in fasting and prayer (v. 21).

Ezra's name means "helper," a characteristic that resides at the heart of good leadership. Under Ezra's prayerful guidance, he and his protégés would lead a spiritual awakening in Jerusalem (see chapters 9–10). All they had needed was a little encouragement and wise direction.

That's how God's church works too. As good mentors encourage and build us up, we learn to do the same for others. Such an influence will reach far beyond our lifetime. Work done faithfully for God stretches into eternity.

MAKING IT WORK

What motivates you in your work for the Lord? Encouragement? Challenge? A biblical admonition? People are motivated in different ways. Use your influence on others in the most impactful way.

_____

_____

_____

_____

_____

_____

_____

_____

_____

_____

_____

_____

_____

_____

_____

_____

_____

_____

_____

Doing the Opposite

COLOSSIANS 2:20–3:4

For you died, and your life
is now hidden with Christ in God.

— COLOSSIANS 3:3

A wilderness excursion can seem daunting, but for outdoor enthusiasts this only adds to the appeal. Because hikers need more water than they can carry, they purchase bottles with built-in filters so they can use water sources along the way. But the process of drinking from such a container is counterintuitive. Tipping the bottle does nothing. A thirsty hiker has to blow into it to force the water through the filter. Reality is contrary to what seems natural.

As we follow Jesus, we find much that is counterintuitive. Paul pointed out one example: Keeping rules won't draw us closer to God. He asked, "Why, as though you still belonged to the world, do you submit to its rules: 'Do not handle! Do not taste! Do not touch!'? These rules . . . are based on merely human commands and teachings" (Colossians 2:20–22).

So what are we to do? Paul gave the answer. "Since, then, you have been raised with Christ, set your hearts on things above" (3:1). "You died," he told people who were still very much alive, "and your life is now hidden with Christ in God" (v. 3).

We are to consider ourselves "dead" to the values of this world and alive to Christ. We now aspire to a way of life demonstrated by the One who said, "Whoever wants to become great among you must be your servant" (Matthew 20:26).

MAKING IT WORK

Today it is so countercultural to live by God's clear biblical guidelines instead of the values of the world. What are some examples of this? How does that affect your decisions about how to live—or the decisions of your children or grandchildren?

_____

_____

_____

_____

_____

_____

_____

_____

_____

_____

_____

_____

_____

_____

_____

_____

_____

_____

_____

The Snake and the Tricycle

LUKE 1:1–4

~~~~~~~

I myself have carefully investigated
everything from the beginning.

—LUKE 1:3

For years, I had retold a story from a time in Ghana when my brother and I were toddlers. As I recalled it, he had parked our old iron tricycle on a small cobra. The trike was too heavy for the snake, which remained trapped under the front wheel.

But after my aunt and my mother had both passed away, we discovered a long-lost letter from Mom recounting the incident. In reality, *I* had parked the tricycle on the snake, and my brother had run to tell Mom. Her eyewitness account, written close to the actual event, revealed the reality.

The historian Luke understood the importance of accurate records. He explained how the story of Jesus was "handed down to us by those who from the first were eyewitnesses" (Luke 1:2). "I too decided to write an orderly account for you," he wrote to Theophilus, "so that you may know the certainty of the things you have been taught" (vv. 3–4). The result was the gospel of Luke. Then, in his introduction to the book of Acts, Luke said of Jesus, "After his suffering, he presented himself to them and gave many convincing proofs that he was alive" (Acts 1:3).

Our faith is not based on hearsay or wishful thinking. It is rooted in the well-documented life of Jesus, who came to give us peace with God. His Story stands.

MAKING IT WORK

Some have referred to Luke as a trustworthy and accurate historian. The fact that he wrote Luke and Acts after thorough research gives authenticity to the facts as he presented them. But that's not all. His words were inspired by the Holy Spirit. What do those facts about Luke's authorship mean to you as you read those two books of the Bible?

_____

_____

_____

_____

_____

_____

_____

_____

_____

_____

_____

_____

_____

_____

_____

_____

_____

Dedicated to Love

ROMANS 9:1–5

~~~~~~~~

My heart's desire and prayer to God
for the Israelites is that they may be saved.

—ROMANS 10:1

As a convert to Jesus Christ, Nabeel Qureshi (1983–2017) wrote books to help his readers understand the people in the religion he left. His tone was respectful, and Qureshi always displayed a heart of love for his people.

Qureshi dedicated one of his books to his sister, who had not yet put her faith in Jesus. The dedication is brief, but powerful. "I am begging God for the day that we can worship him together," he wrote.

We get a sense of that kind of love as we read Paul's letter to the church in Rome. "My heart is filled with bitter sorrow and unending grief," he said, "for my people, my Jewish brothers and sisters. I would be willing to be forever cursed—cut off from Christ!—if that would save them" (Romans 9:2–3 NLT).

Paul loved the Jewish people so much that he would have chosen separation from God if only they would accept Christ. He understood that by rejecting Jesus, his people were rejecting the one true God. This motivated him to appeal to his readers to share the good news of Jesus with everyone (10:14–15).

Today, may we prayerfully dedicate ourselves to the love that aches for those close to us!

MAKING IT WORK

Think for a brief moment about Paul's relatives and friends who knew him and loved him before Jesus saved him. Imagine his agony if they rejected the Savior who radically changed his life. If you have the same concerns, what action needs to be taken?

_____

_____

_____

_____

_____

_____

_____

_____

_____

_____

_____

_____

_____

_____

_____

_____

_____

_____

_____

_____

_____

Every Sparrow Falling

MATTHEW 10:28–33

~~~~~~

Precious in the sight of the Lord
is the death of his faithful servants.

—PSALM 116:15

My mother, so dignified and proper her entire life, now lay in a hospice bed, held captive by debilitating age. Struggling for breath, her declining condition contradicted the gorgeous spring day that danced invitingly on the other side of the windowpane.

All the emotional preparation in the world cannot sufficiently brace us for the stark reality of goodbye. *Death is such an indignity!* I thought.

I diverted my gaze to the birdfeeder outside the window. A grosbeak flitted close to help itself to some seed. Instantly a familiar phrase popped into my mind: "Not a single sparrow can fall to the ground without your Father knowing it" (Matthew 10:29 NLT). Jesus had said that to His disciples as He gave them marching orders for a mission to Judea, but the principle applies to all of us. "You are worth more than many sparrows," He told them (v. 31).

My mom stirred and opened her eyes. Reaching back to her childhood, she used a Dutch term of endearment for her own mother and declared, "Muti's dead!"

"Yes," my wife agreed. "She's with Jesus now." Uncertain, Mom continued. "And Joyce and Jim?" she questioned of her sister and brother. "Yes, they're with Jesus too," said my wife. "But we'll be with them soon!"

"It's hard to wait," Mom said quietly.

MAKING IT WORK

Death stinks. But something makes it bearable for us: the hope that comes with knowing Jesus. How have you experienced that hope in the face of a death of someone close? How does the promise of God's reception of people in heaven give us courage when death hits home?

_____

_____

_____

_____

_____

_____

_____

_____

_____

_____

_____

_____

_____

_____

A Hundred Years from Now

JOB 19:21–27

~~~~~~~

*I know that my redeemer lives, and that
in the end he will stand on the earth.*

—JOB 19:25

"I just want people to remember me a hundred years from now," said screenwriter Rod Serling in 1975. Creator of the TV series *The Twilight Zone*, Serling wanted people to say of him, "He was a writer." Most of us can identify with Serling's desire to leave a legacy—something to give our lives a sense of meaning and permanence.

The story of Job shows us a man struggling with meaning amid life's fleeting days. In a moment, not just his possessions but those most precious to him, his children, were taken. Then his friends accused him of deserving this fate. Job cried out: "Oh, that my words were recorded, that they were written on a scroll, that they were inscribed with an iron tool on lead, or engraved in rock forever!" (Job 19:23–24).

Job's words have been "engraved in rock forever." We have them in the Bible. Yet even Job needed more meaning in his life than the legacy he'd leave behind. He discovered it in the character of God. "I know that my redeemer lives," Job declared, "and that in the end he will stand on the earth" (19:25). This knowledge gave him the right longing. "I myself will see him," Job said. "How my heart yearns within me!" (v. 27).

In the end, Job didn't find what he expected. He found much more—the Source of all meaning and permanence (42:1–6).

MAKING IT WORK

Thousands of years ago, Job found the source of all meaning when He had a close-up encounter with God and His creation. Why do people today so often reject God and the reality of His existence? How do they look at creation and not see what Job saw? What about creation stands out to you as evidence of God's handiwork?

_____

_____

_____

_____

_____

_____

_____

_____

_____

_____

_____

_____

_____

_____

_____

_____

_____

Jesus Picks a Fight

Growing up, my brother and I played sports nearly every day. In Ghana it was the brand of football you play with your feet. Moving to the USA, we quickly learned how to play the other football. And baseball. And basketball. Ice hockey when the millpond froze over.

We wrestled too. And when my brother and I wrestled, it *always* seemed to end in a fistfight. He was bigger and stronger, but I knew the moves.

As I grew older, competing against others helped me learn the discipline of harnessing those volatile emotions. I came to understand that fighting was no way to solve problems.

We can't avoid conflict entirely, however, and some things do seem worth fighting for. But when and how should we fight? Does Jesus give us any answers about that?

We think of Jesus as a man of peace, and that's mostly true. But not entirely. Jesus said of himself, "Don't imagine that I came to bring peace to the earth! I came not to bring peace, but a sword" (Matthew 10:34). He once told His disciples, "If you don't have a sword, sell your cloak and buy one!" (Luke 22:36). In that moment, the disciples actually had two swords, one of which Peter would impulsively use only a few hours later.

Yet, the prophet Isaiah told us the Messiah would be called the Prince of Peace (Isaiah 9:6). And Jesus himself clearly told us to turn the other cheek when we're attacked (Matthew 5:39).

What gives? When do we buy a sword, and when do we turn the other cheek?

Jesus wasn't afraid of a fight. In the last week before His crucifixion, He addressed a crowd within the hearing of powerful religious leaders. He didn't mince words. "Don't follow their example," Jesus said of those leaders. "For they don't practice what they teach. They crush people with unbearable religious demands and never lift a finger to ease the burden" (Matthew 22:3–4).

Jesus was just getting warmed up. "Hypocrites!" He called them (v. 15). "Blind guides!" "Blind fools!" (vv. 16–17). And my personal favorite: "Snakes! Sons of vipers!" (v. 33).

Wait, what? Did Jesus just tell the religious leaders, "Your mothers are vipers"? Seems that way.

This came close on the heels of another fight Jesus had picked. When He entered the Temple, He tipped over tables and chairs and drove out the merchants. He said, "'My Temple will be called a house of prayer,' but you have turned it into a den of thieves!" (Matthew 21:13).

Jesus picked these fights on behalf of others who were being exploited. He couldn't bear to see the religious leaders twisting God's law to give themselves power. Neither could He stand idly by and watch His Father's Temple misused and desecrated by profiteers. He wanted the people to receive His message of repentance, grace, and mercy unhindered by all the human trappings getting in the way.

But Jesus did, in fact, "turn the other cheek" like no one before or after Him. In describing himself as the shepherd of the sheep, Jesus said, "I sacrifice my life so I may take it back again. No one can take my life from me. I sacrifice it voluntarily" (John 10:17–18).

Sheep were a central part of the sacrificial system of the Jewish religion. Yet Jesus, the shepherd, was to be the sacrifice.

As He faced Pilate in history's most notorious trial, Jesus told him, "My Kingdom is not an earthly kingdom. If it were, my followers would fight to keep me from being handed over to the Jewish leaders. But my Kingdom is not of this world" (John 18:36).

This is a principle I tend to forget. In this world, I want to throw punches, metaphoric or otherwise. I want to win for my own selfish reasons.

Jesus shows us another way—a way that will invite misunderstanding and opposition. "If the world hates you," He told His disciples, "remember that it hated me first" (John 15:18). He knew He was about to die, yet He said, "I am not alone because the Father is with me" (16:32). And although He told them, "Here on earth you will have many trials and sorrows," He was quick to add, "but take heart, because I have overcome the world" (16:33).

We're not alone either. But we must remember, it's not about *us* winning. *Jesus* is the one who overcomes the world. And He won't abandon us. We can walk this road together—brother to brother—with the Man who showed us when to pick a fight on behalf of others and when to turn the other cheek.

—TIM

Help us get the word out!

Our Daily Bread Publishing exists to feed the soul with the Word of God.

If you appreciated this book, please let others know.

- Pick up another copy to give as a gift.
- Share a link to the book or mention it on social media.
- Write a review on your blog, on a book-seller's website, or at our own site (odb.org/store).
- Recommend this book for your church, book club, or small group.

Connect with us:

 @ourdailybread

 @ourdailybread

 @ourdailybread

Our Daily Bread Publishing
PO Box 3566
Grand Rapids, Michigan 49501 USA

 books@odb.org

About the Author

As a "third-culture kid" (parents from one culture living in another) Tim Gustafson attended eight different schools in his first nine years of schooling. That doesn't include a "semester at sea" while his adoptive parents took passage to West Africa on a freighter during missionary service. A military veteran of three deployments, Tim and his wife, Leisa, have eight children—seven of whom are boys. They also have what they believe to be the world's most expressive granddaughter. Tim writes for *Our Daily Bread* and serves as an editor for the Discovery Series. To read more from Tim, go to brothertobrother.blog.